Party Food

HOME COOKING

Party Food

BY

THE EDITORS OF TIME-LIFE BOOKS

TIME-LIFE/GEDDES & GROSSET

Contents

Party Food

The sharing of food is the heart and soul of hospitality, and this collection of recipes provides the enterprising party host with a variety of ideas for formal or nonformal entertaining, for a long-planned celebration or an impromptu treat.

Avoiding the usual pit-falls of party food—stodgy dips and fat-laden, over-salted crisps and nuts—this volume presents a more imaginative, and far healthier approach. Using as little butter and salt as possible and avoiding saturated fats, all the recipes have been devised to take full advantage of the rich variety of fresh, natural products available today. Much use is made therefore, of fresh fruit and vegetables; herbs and spices provide a natural source of flavouring, and rich, heavy sauces are abandoned in favour of aromatic marinades and light dressings. Even those party staples which all of us find almost impossible to resist, the savoury titbits, potato crisps and corn chips, can be replaced with more interesting and healthier alternatives – so succumbing to temptation does not always have to mean commiting one of the deadly nutritional sins!

The Key to Better Eating

Home Cooking addresses the concerns of today's weight-conscious, health-minded cooks with recipes that take into account guidelines set by nutritionists. The secret of eating well, of course, has to do with maintaining a balance of foods in the diet. The recipes thus should be used thoughtfully, in the context of a day's eating. To make the choice easier, an analysis is given of nutrients in a single serving. The counts for calories, protein, cholesterol, total fat, saturated fat and sodium are approximate.

Interpreting the chart

The chart below gives dietary guidelines for healthy men, women and children. Recommended figures vary from country to country, but the principles are the same everywhere. Here, the average daily amounts of calories and protein are from a report by the UK Department of Health and Social Security; the maximum advisable daily intake of fat is based on guidelines given by the National Advisory Committee on Nutrition Education (NACNE); those for cholesterol and sodium are based on upper limits suggested by the World Health Organization.

The volumes in the Home Cooking series do not purport to be diet books, nor do they focus on health foods. Rather, they express a common-sense approach to cooking that uses salt, sugar, cream, butter and oil in moderation while employing other ingredients that also provide flavour and satisfaction. The portions themselves are modest in size.

The recipes make few unusual demands. Naturally they call for fresh ingredients, offering substitutes when these are unavailable. (The substitute is not calculated in the nutrient analysis, however.)

Most of the ingredients can be found in any well-stocked supermarket.

Heavy-bottomed pots and pans are recommended to guard against burning whenever a small amount of oil is used and where there is danger of the food adhering to the hot surface, but non-stick pans can be utilized as well. Both safflower oil and virgin olive oil are favoured for sautéing. Safflower oil was chosen because it is the most highly polyunsaturated vegetable fat available in supermarkets, and polyunsaturated fats reduce blood cholesterol; if unobtainable, use sunflower oil, also high in polyunsaturated fats. Virgin olive oil is used because it has a fine fruity flavour lacking in the lesser grade known as 'pure'. In addition, it is—like all olive oil—high in mono-unsaturated fats, which are thought not to increase blood cholesterol. When virgin olive oil is unavailable, or when its flavour is not essential to the success of the dish, 'pure' may be used.

About cooking times

To help planning, time is taken into account in the recipes. While recognizing that everyone cooks at a different speed and that stoves and ovens differ, approximate 'working' and 'total' times are provided. Working time stands for the minutes actively spent on preparation; total time includes unattended cooking time, as well as time devoted to marinating, steeping or soaking ingredients. Since the recipes emphasize fresh foods, they may take a bit longer to prepare than 'quick and easy' dishes that call for canned or packaged products, but the difference in flavour, and often in nutrition, should compensate for the little extra time involved.

Recommended Dietary Guidelines

Average Daily Intake			Maximum Daily Intake			
	Calories	Protein grams	Cholesterol milligrams	Total fat grams	Saturated fat grams	Sodium milligrams
Females 7-8	1900	47	300	80	32	2000*
9-11	2050	51	300	77	35	2000
12-17	2150	53	300	81	36	2000
18-54	2150	54	300	81	36	2000
55-74	1900	47	300	72	32	2000
Males 7-8	1980	49	300	80	33	2000
9-11	2280	57	300	77	38	2000
12-14	2640	66	300	99	44	2000
15-17	2880	72	300	108	48	2000
18-34	2900	72	300	109	48	2000
35-64	2750	69	300	104	35	2000
65-74	2400	60	300	91	40	2000

* (or 5g salt)

Almond and Persimmon Stars

Makes 12 stars
Working time: about 30 minutes
Total time: about 1 hour and 10 minutes
Per star: Calories 60, Protein 1g, Cholesterol 0mg, Total
fat 5g, Saturated,fat 1g, Sodium 35mg

1	sheet phyllo pastry, about 45 by 30 cm (18 by 12 inches)
30 g/1 oz	polyunsaturated margarine, melted
2	persimmons, peeled, one chopped, one sliced
3 tbsp	ground almonds
2 tbsp	ground amaretti biscuits
1	egg white

Grease and lightly flour twelve 7.5 cm (3 inch) shallow, flat-based tartlet tins. Preheat the oven to 200°C (400°F or Mark 6).

Spread the phyllo out on a work surface and brush it with the melted margarine. Cut the sheet into twenty-four 7.5 cm (3 inch) squares. Line each tartlet tin with two squares of phyllo, arranging the corners to form an eight-pointed star.

To make the filling, purée the chopped persimmon in a blender or food processor. Transfer the purée to a mixing bowl and stir in the ground almonds and amaretti biscuit crumbs. In a separate bowl, whisk the egg white until it is stiff, then fold it gently into the persimmon-amaretti mixture.

Distribute the filling among the phyllo stars and bake them until the pastry is golden—15 to 20 minutes. Allow the stars to cool briefly in their tins, then unmould them on to wire racks to cool completely.

Decorate each star with the slices of persimmon. Serve the stars on the day they are baked, while the pastry is still crisp.

EDITOR'S NOTE: If amaretti biscuits are unobtainable, crumbled almond macaroons, or any other crumbled sweet biscuits, may be substituted.

Almond Petits Fours with Kumquat and Ginger

Makes: 30 petits fours
Working time: about 30 minutes
Total time: about 50 minutes
Per petit four: Calories 60, Protein 1g, Cholesterol 0mg, Total fat 4g, Saturated fat 1g, Sodium 5mg

125 g/4 oz	*caster sugar, plus 2 teaspoons for the glaze*
2	*egg whites, lightly beaten*
175 g/6 oz	*ground almonds*
1	*orange, finely grated rind and juice*
1/4 tsp	*pure vanilla extract*
5	*kumquats, sliced and seeded*
2 tsp	*diced preserved stem ginger*

Preheat the oven to 180°C (350°F or Mark 4). Line a baking sheet with non-stick parchment paper.

In a mixing bowl, combine the 125 g (4 oz) of caster sugar with the egg whites, ground almonds, orange rind and vanilla extract to form a soft paste. Transfer the mixture to a piping bag fitted with a 2 cm (³/₄ inch) star nozzle and pipe 30 small rosettes on to the parchment paper. Decorate the top of each rosette with one slice of kumquat and a little diced ginger. Bake the petits fours in the oven until they are golden-brown— about 20 minutes.

Meanwhile, prepare the glaze. Put the orange juice and the remaining sugar in a small saucepan. Heat gently, stirring until the sugar has dissolved, then increase the heat and boil the mixture rapidly for 3 to 4 minutes until it becomes syrupy.

While the petits fours are still warm, paint the orange glaze over the kumquat and ginger. Allow to cool before serving.

Almond Spirals

Makes 18 spirals
Working time: about 35 minutes
Total time: about 50 minutes
Per spiral: Calories 85, Protein 2g, Cholesterol trace, Total
fat 6g, Saturated fat 2g, Sodium 5mg

125 g/4 oz	*ground almonds*
90 g/3 oz	*caster sugar*
1	*egg white*
1/4 tsp	*pure almond extract*
6	*sheets phyllo pastry, each about 45 by 30 cm (18 by 12 inches)*
45 g/1 1/2 oz	*unsalted butter, melted*
	icing sugar, to decorate

In a mixing bowl, combine the ground almonds, caster sugar, egg white and almond extract to give a smooth paste. Divide the paste into 18 equal portions.

Cut each sheet of phyllo widthwise into three equal rectangles measuring 30 by 15 cm (12 by 6 inches). Stack all 18 rectangles in one pile, then cover them with a clean, damp cloth.

Preheat the oven to 190°C (375°F or Mark 5).

Assemble the spirals one at a time to prevent the phyllo from drying out. Take a portion of almond paste and roll it on a work surface into a 29 cm (11 1/2 inch) long, thin sausage. If the paste sticks, powder the work surface with a little icing sugar. Place a sheet of phyllo on the worktop and brush with a little melted butter, then place the roll of almond paste along one long edge of the pastry. Roll up the phyllo, enclosing the almond filling, then shape the roll into a spiral. Repeat this process until all the portions of almond paste and phyllo rectangles have been made into spirals.

Arrange the phyllo spirals on baking trays, pressing the loose ends against the sides of the trays in order to prevent them from unrolling. Brush each spiral with melted butter, then bake them for 12 to 15 minutes, until golden-brown.

Remove the spirals from the oven and cool them on wire racks. Before serving, sift a little icing sugar over each pastry to decorate.

Apricot and Hazelnut Petits Fours

THIS RECIPE IS IDEAL FOR USING UP GENOESE SPONGE TRIMMINGS THAT MAY BE LEFT OVER.

Makes 24 petits fours
Working time: about 20 minutes
Total time: about 1 hour and 20 minutes (includes chilling)
Per petit four: Calories 35, Protein 1g, Cholesterol 10mg,
Total fat 2g, Saturated fat 0g, Sodium 20mg

125 g/4 oz	*genoese sponge or other plain sponge cake*
60 g/2 oz	*dried apricots, finely chopped*
30 g/1 oz	*shelled hazelnuts, toasted and skinned, finely chopped or coarsely ground*
2 tbsp	*orange-flavoured liqueur*
2 tbsp	*apricot jam without added sugar*
2 tsp	*icing sugar*

Place the sponge cake in a food processor or blender and process it into crumbs; alternatively, rub the sponge cake through a wire sieve. Put the crumbs into a mixing bowl with the chopped apricots, hazelnuts, orange-flavoured liqueur and apricot jam, and mix them well together.

Gather up the mixture in your hands and roll it out, using your palms, into a long, thin roll. Flatten the top and sides of the roll a little, then cut it into 24 equal slices. Lay the slices flat on the work surface and sift the icing sugar over them.

Place each slice in a petit four case. Chill the petits fours for at least 1 hour before serving.

Baby Courgettes Vinaigrette

Serves 4
Working (and total) time: about 15 minutes
Calories 90, Protein 1g, Cholesterol 0mg, Total fat 8g,
Saturated fat 1g, Sodium 200mg

500 g/1 lb	*baby courgettes*
1	*garlic clove, finely chopped*
1/4 tsp	*salt*
1 tsp	*grainy mustard*
1/2 tsp	*Dijon mustard*
	freshly ground black pepper
1 tbsp	*white wine vinegar*
2 tbsp	*virgin olive oil*
7	*purple basil leaves, torn*

With a sharp knife slice the courgettes diagonally into 2.5 cm (1 inch) pieces and plunge them into a saucepan filled with boiling water. Boil the courgettes until they are just tender—about 5 minutes.

While the courgettes cook, prepare the dressing. Place the garlic and the salt in a mortar and pound them with a pestle until the garlic has broken down into a purée. Mix in the two mustards, the pepper and the vinegar, then whisk in the olive oil.

Remove the courgettes from the heat, drain them in a colander, and refresh them quickly under cold running water to arrest their cooking. Drain them thoroughly again.

Transfer the drained courgettes on to a shallow serving dish. Toss them with the mustard dressing and the basil leaves, and serve the salad immediately.

EDITOR'S NOTE: If purple basil is unavailable, use ordinary fresh basil leaves instead.

Bacon and Monkfish Rolls

Makes 18 rolls
Working time: about 15 minutes
Total time: about 45 minutes (includes marinating)
Per roll: Calories 70, Protein 6g, Cholesterol 25mg, Total fat 5g, Saturated fat 2g, Sodium 110mg

500 g/1 lb	*trimmed, skinned and boned monkfish or halibut*
1/2 tsp	*finely chopped fresh thyme*
1	*bay leaf, broken*
	freshly ground black pepper
1	*lemon, juice only*
9	*thin rashers back bacon, trimmed of fat, cut in half lengthwise*

Cut the fish into 18 cubes and put these in a bowl with the thyme, bay leaf, some pepper and the lemon juice.

Turn the cubes to coat them well and leave to marinate for at least 30 minutes. Meanwhile, soak 18 short wooden cocktail sticks in cold water for 10 minutes to prevent them from scorching under the grill.

Discard the pieces of bay leaf from the fish marinade. Wrap each cube of fish with a piece of bacon and thread on to a stick; ensure that the skewers pierce through the overlapping ends of bacon, to hold them together.

Cook the rolls under a hot grill for 4 to 5 minutes, turning once. Serve immediately.

Barquettes with Three Fillings

Serves 6

Working time: about 1 hour

Total time: about 2 hours and 15 minutes (includes chilling)

Calories 260, Protein 12g, Cholesterol 40mg, Total fat 15g, Saturated fat 4g, Sodium 490mg

125 g/4 oz	*plain flour*
1/8 tsp	*salt*
60 g/2 oz	*polyunsaturated margarine*
1/2	*beaten egg*

Smoked mackerel mousse

175 g/6 oz	*smoked mackerel fillet, skinned and any bones removed*
15 g/1/2 oz	*polyunsaturated margarine*
1/4 tsp	*salt*
	freshly ground black pepper
2 tsp	*fresh lemon juice*
3	*thin slices of lemon, cut into quarters*

Asparagus cream

175 g/6 oz	*thin asparagus spears, trimmed*
1 tbsp	*soured cream*
1/8 tsp	*salt*
	freshly ground black pepper

Prawn salad

1 tsp	*virgin olive oil*
1 tsp	*wine vinegar*
1	*garlic clove, crushed*
2 tsp	*finely chopped parsley*
	freshly ground black pepper
90 g/3 oz	*peeled prawns*
2	*lettuce leaves, washed, dried and shredded*

To make the pastry, sift the flour and salt into a mixing bowl. Rub the margarine into the flou runtil the mixture resembles fine breadcrumbs. Mix the dry ingredients together with the beaten egg and 1 to 2 tablespoons of cold water to make a firm dough.

On a floured surface, roll the dough out very thinly. Cut it into strips long and wide enough to line eighteen 9.5 cm (3³/₄ inch) long barquette tins. (If you do not have that many tins, bake the pastry cases in batches.) Prick the dough all over with a fork, then place the tins on a baking sheet and refrigerate for 30 minutes. Preheat the oven to 220°C (425°F or Mark 7).

Bake the pastry cases until they are very lightly browned—10 to 15 minutes. Carefully remove the pastry cases from the tins and transfer them to a wire rack to cool while you prepare the three fillings.

To make the smoked mackerel mousse, flake the fish and put it into a food processor or blender with the margarine, salt, some pepper and the lemon juice. Blend until the mixture is smooth and creamy. Spoon the filling into a small bowl, cover it with plastic film and place it in the refrigerator to chill.

To make the asparagus cream, boil the asparagus in 2.5 cm (1 inch) of water in a frying pan, until tender—about 3 minutes. Drain the spears and refresh them under cold running water. When cool, remove the tips from six of the spears and set them aside to use as a garnish. Finely chop the remaining asparagus and put it in a small bowl. Add the soured cream, salt and some pepper, and mix well. Cover the filling with plastic film and place it in the refrigerator.

To make the prawn salad, put the oil, vinegar, garlic and parsley into a small bowl, season with pepper and stir well. Mix the prawns with this dressing, cover with plastic film and refrigerate with the two other fillings. Chill all three fillings for at least 1 hour.

To complete the barquettes, remove the fillings from the refrigerator about 20 to 30 minutes before serving. Spoon the smoked mackerel mousse into six boats and garnish with the lemon pieces. Fill another six boats with the asparagus cream and top with the reserved asparagus tips. Fill the remaining boats with a little shredded lettuce, topped with the prawns.

Buckwheat Blinis with Caviare

THESE LITTLE PANCAKES, USUALLY PARTNERED WITH CAVIARE TO MAKE A CLASSIC RUSSIAN HORS-D'OEUVRE, ARE HERE GARNISHED WITH LOW FAT *FROMAGE FRAIS* INSTEAD OF SOURED CREAM.

Serves 10

Working time: about 30 minutes

Total time: about 2 hours and 30 minutes

Calories 145, Protein 11g, Cholesterol 85mg, Total fat 6g, Saturated fat 3g, Sodium 325mg

1 tsp	*caster sugar*
2 tsp	*dried yeast*
300 g/10 oz	*buckwheat flour*
1/4 tsp	*salt*
35 cl/12 fl oz	*tepid milk*
1	*egg, separated, plus one egg white*
125 g/4 oz	*caviare or black lumpfish roe*
500 g/1 lb	*fromage frais*
6	*spring onions, chopped*

Combine the sugar and 15 cl (1/4 pint) of tepid water in a bowl and stir to dissolve the sugar, then whisk in the dried yeast until it has dissolved. Add the buckwheat flour and the salt, and mix well, then whisk in the tepid milk and the egg yolk. Cover the bowl and leave the batter in a warm place to rise until it has doubled in bulk—1 1/2 to 2 hours.

Whisk the yeast batter lightly until it becomes liquid again. In another bowl, whisk the egg whites until they are stiff. Fold them into the batter with a metal spoon. Let the batter stand for 10 minutes.

Heat a non-stick frying pan or griddle over medium heat. Drop the batter from a large spoon on to the pan to make little pancakes about 6 cm (2 1/2 inches) in diameter. Cook the blinis until they are golden-brown on both sides—1 1/2 to 2 minutes in all. As the blinis cook, remove them from the pan and keep them hot in a folded tea towel.

Top each blini with a teaspoon of the caviare or lumpfish roe, a tablespoon of the *fromage frais* and a generous sprinkling of the spring onions. Serve hot.

EDITOR'S NOTE: Buckwheat flour is more variable in consistency than other sorts of flour. When combining it with milk, you may have to alter the quantity of liquid specified here to produce a batter that drops easily from a spoon.

Bacon and Onion Potato Salad

Serves 6 as a side dish
Working time: about 10 minutes
Total time: about 20 minutes
Calories 140, Protein 3g, Cholesterol 2mg, Total fat 2g,
Saturated fat 0g, Sodium 45mg

1 kg/2 lb	*small round red potatoes of equal size, scrubbed*
2	*rashers bacon, cut into thin strips*
1	*red onion, thinly sliced*
4 tbsp	*finely chopped celery*
1 tbsp	*cornflour, mixed with 12.5 cl (4 fl oz) unsalted chicken stock*
4 tbsp	*white vinegar*
	freshly ground black pepper
2 tbsp	*coarsely chopped parsley*

Prick the potatoes with a fork in two places; any more punctures would let too much moisture escape.

Arrange them in a circle on absorbent paper towel in the microwave oven; cook them on high for 7 minutes. Turn the potatoes over and rearrange them; con-tinue cooking them on high until they are barely soft—5 to 7 minutes more. Remove the potatoes from the oven and set them aside until they are cool enough to handle.

Put the bacon strips in a bowl; cover the bowl with a paper towel and microwave the bacon on high for 2 minutes. Remove the towel and drain off the excess fat, then add the onion and celery to the bowl. Toss the bacon and vegetables together, cover the bowl, and microwave on high for 90 seconds. Stir in the cornflour mixture and the vinegar. Cover the bowl and microwave it on high until the dressing thickens slightly—about 2 minutes.

Cut the potatoes into slices about 5 mm ($^1\!/_4$ inch) thick. Pour the dressing over the potato slices; add a generous grinding of pepper and half the parsley. Gently toss the salad, then cool somewhat. Scatter the remaining parsley over the top just before serving.

Chilled Tomato and Prawn Soup

Serves 4

Working time: about 20 minutes

Total time: about 1 hour and 20 minutes (includes chilling)

Calories 120, Protein 14g, Cholesterol 95mg, Total fat 1g,
Saturated fat 0g, Sodium 150mg

1/2 litre/16 fl oz	*unsalted veal or chicken stock*
4	*tomatoes, skinned, seeded, chopped*
1/2	*cucumber, peeled, seeded, chopped*
1	*spring onion trimmed and sliced*
2 tbsp	*red wine vinegar*
1/4 tsp	*white pepper*
1 tsp	*Dijon mustard*
4 to 8	*drops Tabasco sauce*
350 g/12 oz	*cooked peeled prawns or shrimps*
	croûtons (optional)

Pour the stock into a serving bowl. Stir in the tomatoes, cucumber, spring onion, vinegar, pepper, mustard and Tabasco sauce. Add the prawns and stir again. Cover the bowl and refrigerate it for at least 1 hour. Serve the soup in chilled soup bowls; if you wish, garnish each portion with a few croûtons.

Chocolate Kisses

Makes 36 kisses
Working time: about 40 minutes
Total time: about 50 minutes
Per kiss: Calories 65, Protein 1g, Cholesterol 0mg, Total
fat 2g, Saturated fat 1g, Sodium 5mg

60 g/2 oz	plain chocolate, broken into pieces
125 g/4 oz	blanched almonds, toasted and finely ground
125 g/4 oz	shelled hazelnuts, toasted and skinned, finely ground
90 g/3 oz	cornmeal
90 g/3 oz	icing sugar
90 g/3 oz	caster sugar
1 tbsp	clear honey
2	egg whites
5 tbsp	apricot jam without added sugar

Preheat the oven to 220°C (425°F or Mark 7). Line two large baking sheets with non-stick parchment paper.

Melt the chocolate in a heatproof bowl set over a pan of simmering water. Place the almonds, hazelnuts, cornmeal, icing sugar, caster sugar and honey in a mixing bowl. Pour on the melted chocolate and stir the mixture thoroughly, then add the egg whites and stir again until a stiff batter is formed.

Spoon the mixture into a piping bag fitted with a 5 mm (¼ inch) star nozzle. Pipe 72 rosettes, each about 4 cm (1½ inches) in diameter, at least 2.5 cm (1 inch) apart, on to the prepared baking sheets.

Bake the rosettes until they are set—8 to 10 minutes—then transfer them to wire racks and leave them to cool. Just before serving, sandwich the rosettes together in pairs, using the jam as filling.

EDITOR'S NOTE: To toast almonds, put them on a baking sheet under a hot grill for 2 to 3 minutes, or until golden; turn or shake them constantly.

Chocolate-Dipped Meringue Fingers

Makes 60 fingers
Working time: about 35 minutes
Total time: about 2 hours

Per finger: Calories 35, Protein trace, Cholesterol 0mg,
Total fat 2g, Saturated fat 1g, Sodium 10mg

2	egg whites
125 g/4 oz	caster sugar
1 tbsp	cocoa powder
1/2 tsp	grated orange rind, thoroughly dried on kitchen paper
150 g/5 oz	plain chocolate
150 g/5 oz	white chocolate

Preheat the oven to 130°C (250°F or Mark 1/2). Line two baking sheets with non-stick parchment paper.

Whisk the egg whites until they form soft peaks. Add half the sugar and continue whisking until the mixture is stiff and glossy. Using a metal spoon, gently fold in the remaining sugar. Divide the stiffly beaten whites into two equal parts. Flavour one half with the cocoa powder and the other with the orange rind, folding the latter in very gently so as not to "break" the meringue.

Transfer one of the meringue mixtures to a piping bag fitted with a 1 cm (1/2 inch) plain nozzle. Pipe 7.5 cm (3 inch) fingers, spaced at least 2.5 cm (1 inch) apart on to one of the prepared baking sheets. Repeat the process with the second batch of meringue. Bake the fingers until they are completely dry—about 1 hour—then transfer them to wire racks to cool.

Melt the plain chocolate with 4 tablespoons of water in a heatproof bowl set over a pan of simmering water. Half-ice the orange-flavoured fingers by dipping them at an angle into the melted chocolate. Leave them to set on a sheet of non-stick parchment paper. Meanwhile, melt the white chocolate and coat the cocoa-flavoured fingers in the same way.

EDITOR'S NOTE: Meringue fingers may be stored in an airtight tin in a cool, dry place for several days.

Chocolate-Tipped Horseshoes

Makes 30 horseshoes
Working time: about 30 minutes
Total time: about 1 hour
Per horseshoe: Calories 100, Protein 1g, Cholesterol
25mg, Total fat 5g, Saturated fat 3g, Sodium 75mg

125 g/4 oz *unsalted butter*
100 g/3¹/₂ oz *icing sugar, sifted*
2 *egg yolks*
1 tsp *pure vanilla extract*
175 g/6 oz *plain flour*
90 g/3 oz *cornmeal*
45 g/1¹/₂ oz *plain chocolate, broken into pieces*
45 g/1¹/₂ oz *white chocolate, broken into pieces*

Preheat the oven to 170°C (325°F or Mark 3). Line
two large baking sheets with non-stick parchment paper.

Beat the butter and sugar together in a mixing bowl
until light and fluffy. Beat in the egg yolks and vanilla
extract, sift in the flour and cornmeal, and continue to
beat until the ingredients are thoroughly combined.

Take a piece of the dough and roll it between the
palms of your hands into a rope about 1 cm (¹/₂ inch)
thick. Cut the rope into 10 cm (4 inch) lengths, then
curve each piece into a horseshoe shape and place it
on the baking parchment. Roll and shape the remaining dough in the same way, spacing the horseshoes
well apart on the parchment to allow for spreading.
There should be 30 horseshoes in all.

Bake the horseshoes until they are lightly
browned—15 to 20 minutes—then transfer them to
wire racks and let them cool.

Melt the plain and white chocolate in separate
heatproof bowls set over pans of simmering water.
Dip the ends of half of the horseshoes in the plain
chocolate and the remaining horseshoes in the white
chocolate. Place them on a tray lined with non-stick
parchment paper and let the chocolate set before
serving.

Cold Apple and Tarragon Soup

Serves 4

Working (and total) time: about 1 hour and 20 minutes
(includes chilling)

Calories 150, Protein 4g, Cholesterol 10mg, Total fat 4g,
Saturated fat 2g, Sodium 130mg

7 g/¼ oz	unsalted butter
1 tbsp	finely chopped shallot
600 g/1¼ lb	tart apples, peeled, cored and sliced
2 tbsp	chopped fresh tarragon
30 cl/½ pint	unsalted chicken stock
17.5 cl/6 fl oz	unsweetened apple juice
¼ tsp	white pepper
⅛ tsp	salt
	grated nutmeg
¼ litre/8 fl oz	semi-skimmed milk
	tarragon sprigs for garnish (optional)

Put the butter into a 2 litre (3½ pint) bowl. Cover the bowl with plastic film or a lid, and microwave the butter on high until it has melted—about 30 seconds. Add the shallot and stir to coat it with the butter. Cover the bowl again and cook the shallot on medium high (70 per cent power) until it is translucent—about 45 seconds. Add the apples, tarragon, stock, apple juice, pepper, salt and a pinch of nutmeg. Cover the bowl, leaving one corner open, and cook the mixture on high until the apples are soft—about 6 minutes.

Purée the contents of the bowl in a blender, food processor or food mill. Return the soup to the bowl and refrigerate it for at least 1 hour, then stir in the milk. Garnish the soup with the tarragon sprigs, if you are using them, and serve immediately.

Exotic Fruit Salad

Serves 12
Working (and total) time: about 40 minutes
Calories 115, Protein 3g, Cholesterol 0mg, Total fat 2g,
Saturated fat trace, Sodium 60mg

6 *ripe passion fruits*
2 *small green-fleshed melons, halved and seeded, flesh scooped into balls with a melon-baller*
1 *pink-fleshed melon, halved and seeded, flesh scooped into balls with a melon-baller*
1 *pineapple, peeled and cored, flesh cut into chunks*
3 *guavas, halved lengthwise, seeded, each half sliced crosswise*
2 *pink grapefruits, peeled and segmented*
3 *papayas, peeled and seeded, flesh cut into chunks*
2 *large mangoes, peeled, flesh cut lengthwise into slices, stones discarded*

Cut the passion fruits in half crosswise. Using a teaspoon, scoop out the seeds and pulp from each passion fruit into a fine nylon sieve set over a bowl. Using the back of the spoon, press all the juice through the sieve into the bowl; discard the seeds and fibrous pulp remaining in the sieve.

Place all the prepared fruits in a large serving bowl and pour the passion fruit juice over them. Gently mix and turn the fruits in the bowl, to ensure that they are all coated with juice. Store the fruit salad in the refrigerator until you are ready to serve it.

EDITOR'S NOTE. The skin of a ripe passion fruit is very dark in colour and has a wrinkled, shrivelled appearance. Avoid any fruits that have paler, plumper-looking skins; the flesh will taste bitter and acidic.

East-West Crab and Vegetable Crescents

Serves 12

Working (and total) time: about 1 hour and 45 minutes

Calories 190, Protein 10g, Cholesterol 80mg, Total fat 4g, Saturated fat 1g, Sodium 150mg

250 g/8 oz	*strong plain flour*
1/4 tsp	*salt*
1 tbsp	*safflower oil*
2	*eggs*
1/8 tsp	*saffron threads (loosely packed), macerated for 20 minutes in 10 cl (3 1/2 fl oz) boiling water*
	Vegetable and crab filling
1 tbsp	*safflower oil*
3	*spring onions, white and green parts separated and finely chopped*
185 g/6 1/2 oz	*bamboo shoots, finely diced*
2	*parsnips, parboiled for 10 minutes, drained and finely diced*
20 g/3/4 oz	*dried shiitake mushrooms, soaked in 12.5 cl (4 fl oz) cold water for 20 minutes*
7 g/1/4 oz	*dried ceps, soaked in 4 tbsp cold water for 20 minutes*
1 tbsp	*miso*
1	*garlic clove, finely chopped*
2 tsp	*finely grated fresh ginger root*
125 g/4 oz	*button mushrooms, finely diced*
1 tsp	*dry sherry*
1 tsp	*low-sodium soy sauce or shoyu*
1/8 tsp	*cayenne pepper*
	freshly ground black pepper
250 g/8 oz	*fresh crab meat, picked over and flaked*
90 g/3 oz	*fresh coriander*

To make the dough for the dumplings, sieve the flour and the salt on to a cool, lightly floured work surface. Make a well in the centre of the flour, and pour in the oil and the eggs. Pour the saffron water through a small strainer into the well; transfer the saffron threads to a small bowl, and cover them with 2 tablespoons of boiling water.

With your fingertips, work the flour mixture into a soft dough. If the mixture is too dry, add a little more strained saffron water. Knead the dough until it is smooth and elastic, cover it with an inverted bowl, and leave it to rest for 1 hour.

While the dough rests, prepare the filling. In a wok or a heavy frying pan, heat 1/2 tablespoon of the oil over medium heat and stir-fry the white part of the spring onions until soft—about 30 seconds. Add the bamboo shoots and stir-fry for 1 minute, then add the parsnips and stir-fry for 30 seconds more. Remove the vegetables from the wok and set them aside.

Remove the shiitake mushrooms and the ceps from their soaking liquids with a slotted spoon and finely chop them. Strain the soaking liquids through a fine-meshed sieve into a bowl and stir in the miso.

Heat the remaining oil in the wok, toss in the garlic and the ginger and stir-fry until they are slightly golden; add the ceps, shiitake and button mushrooms and stir-fry for another minute. Pour in the miso mixture, increase the heat, and stir-fry until the liquid is nearly absorbed. Add the sherry, soy sauce, cayenne and some black pepper. Reduce the heat and cook until the mushrooms are dry—about 30 seconds. Remove the wok from the heat. In a large bowl, combine the stir-fried vegetables, the crab meat and the chopped spring onion greens, and set the mixture aside to cool.

Meanwhile, on a floured work surface, divide the dough into four parts with a sharp knife, and roll out each portion as thinly as possible. Using a 7.5 cm (3 inch) round, fluted pastry cutter, cut 15 circles of dough from each sheet.

Using a pastry brush, paint one half of a dough circle with cold water. Put 1 heaped teaspoon of filling on the unmoistened half-circle and place a coriander leaf, shiny side down, on the other half. Fold over the dough to cover the filling and pinch the edges of the circle together to seal them. Bend the dumpling gently into a crescent-moon shape and leave it to dry on a lightly oiled baking sheet. Repeat the process to fill and shape the remaining dumplings.

To cook the dumplings, bring about 2 litres (3 1/2 pints) of water to the boil in a large pan. Add a drop of oil and a pinch of salt, adjust the heat so that the water is just bubbling, and lower 12 to 18 of the crescents carefully into the pan. Poach the dumplings until they float to the surface, then remove them with a slotted spoon. Set them aside in a warm place while you poach the remaining crescents.

Serve the dumplings hot.

Fig Flowers

Makes 16 flowers
Working time: about 40 minutes
Total time: about 1 hour and 20 minutes
Per flower: Calories 105, Protein 2g, Cholesterol 0mg,
Total fat 7g, Saturated fat 1g, Sodium 80mg

150 g/5 oz	*plain flour*
30 g/1 oz	*cornmeal*
1 tsp	*caster sugar*
90 g/3 oz	*polyunsaturated margarine, chilled*
1	*egg white*

Creamy fig filling

5	*ripe figs, quartered lengthwise*
125 g/4 oz	*medium-fat soft cheese*
1 tbsp	*plain low-fat yoghurt*
1 tsp	*rose-water*
1 tsp	*sugar*

To make the dough, sift the flour, cornmeal and sugar into a mixing bowl, then rub in the margarine with your fingertips until the mixture resembles fine breadcrumbs Mix in the egg white with a round-bladed knife, then gather the dough into a ball and knead it briefly on a lightly floured surface until smooth.

Roll the dough out to a thickness of about 3 mm (1/8 inch) and cut out 16 shapes with a 7.5 cm (3 inch) flower cutter. Fit the shapes into 7. 5 cm (3 inch) tartlet tins, easing the dough across the base and up the sides of the tins without spoiling the petals. Prick the insides with a fork and chill the flower-shaped cases for 30 minutes. Meanwhile, preheat the oven to 190°C (375°F or Mark 5).

Bake the tartlet cases until they are lightly browned at the edges—7 to 10 minutes. Allow them to cool slightly, then turn them out on to a wire rack and leave them to cool fully.

To fill the tartlets, cut the fig quarters lengthwise into thin slices, and arrange the slices in the pastry flowers to look like petals. Using a wooden spoon, mix together the soft cheese, yoghurt, rose-water and sugar until the mixture becomes smooth and creamy. Transfer the cheese mixture to a piping bag fitted with a 5 mm (1/4 inch) star nozzle and pipe a mound of filling into the centre of each fig flower.

Fruit and Nut Triangles

Serves 6

Working time: about 25 minutes

Total time: about 45 minutes

Calories 205, Protein 4g, Cholesterol 0mg, Total fat 12g,
Saturated fat 5g, Sodium 100mg

90 g/3 oz *plain flour*
1 tbsp *caster sugar*
60 g/2 oz *polyunsaturated margarine*
15 g/¹/₂ oz *shelled walnuts, chopped*
15 g/¹/₂ oz *pine-nuts, chopped*
15 g/¹/₂ oz *shelled pistachio nuts, chopped*
20 g/³/₄ oz *semolina*
2 tbsp *clear honey*
60 g/2 oz *sultanas*
30 g/1 oz *stoned dried dates, chopped*
30 g/1 oz *dried apricots, chopped*
1 tsp *rose-water*
1 *shelled walnut half, for decoration*

Preheat the oven to 200°C (400°F or Mark 6). Lightly grease and flour a 20 cm (8 inch) diameter loose bottomed sandwich tin.

Sift the flour and sugar into a large bowl, and rub in the margarine with your fingertips until the mixture resembles breadcrumbs. Using a round-bladed knife, mix 1¹/₂ teaspoons of iced water into the dry ingredients to form a soft dough. Gather the dough into a ball and knead it briefly on a lightly floured work surface, to smooth it. Alternatively, you can prepare the dough in a food processor.

Press the dough evenly into the base of the prepared sandwich tin, and prick it all over with a fork. Spread out all the chopped nuts on a baking sheet. Cook the nuts and the pastry base in the oven for 10 minutes, stirring the nuts occasionally. Remove the nuts and pastry case from the oven, but leave the oven switched on. Run a sharp knife round the edge of the pastry base, to loosen it.

While the pastry and nuts are cooking, prepare the topping. Place the semolina, honey, sultanas, dates and apricots in a small, heavy-bottomed saucepan with 15 cl (¹/₄ pint) of water. Stir the ingredients together and bring them just to the boil. Reduce the heat and simmer the mixture for about 8 minutes, or until it has formed a thick purée. Remove the pan from the heat and stir in the rose-water and the roasted nuts. Spread the fruit and nut filling over the pastry base in an even layer and return it to the oven for 20 minutes.

Allow the baked sweet pastry to cool in its tin, then cut it into 12 triangles. Cover the tin with plastic film and store the triangles in the refrigerator. At the party, arrange the triangles on a round serving dish and place the walnut half in the centre.

Fruit-Filled Gems

GEMS ARE MINIATURE MUFFINS; MINI BUN TINS ARE AVAILABLE AT
GOURMET AND PROFESSIONAL KITCHEN EQUIPMENT STORES.

Makes 24 gems
Working time: about 45 minutes
Total time: about 1 hour and 15 minutes
Per gem: Calories 83, Protein 1g, Cholesterol 15mg, Total
fat 3g, Saturated fat 1g, Sodium 30mg

1	*cooking apple, peeled, cored and coarsely grated*
75 g/2½ oz	*dried apricots, chopped*
12.5 cl/4 fl oz	*unsweetened apple juice*
1	*lemon, grated rind and juice*
150 g/5 oz	*caster sugar*
175 g/6 oz	*plain flour*
¼ tsp	*baking powder*
30 g/1 oz	*unsalted butter*
30 g/1 oz	*unsalted polyunsaturated margarine*
1	*egg, beaten*
2 tbsp	*chopped almonds, toasted*

Combine the apple, apricots, apple juice, lemon rind and juice, and 4 tablespoons of the sugar in a non-reactive saucepan and bring the mixture to the boil. Reduce the heat and simmer the mixture until the fruit is soft and most of the juice has evaporated—about 15 minutes. Set the filling aside and let it cool.

Combine the remaining sugar with the flour and baking powder in a bowl. Cut the butter and margarine into the dry ingredients with a pastry blender or two knives until the mixture resembles coarse meal. With your fingertips, work the egg into the dough just until the egg is incorporated and the dough begins to hold together. Shape two thirds of the dough into a log about 2.5 cm (1 inch) wide, wrap it in plastic film and chill it for 15 minutes. Shape the remaining dough into a round about 1 cm (1½ inch) thick; wrap and chill it.

Preheat the oven to 180°C (350°F or Mark 4).

Cut the dough log into 24 pieces and flatten each one slightly. Press one of the pieces into a 4 cm (1½ inch) cup of a mini bun tin to line it, moulding the dough along the sides to the top of the cup. Use the remaining pieces of dough to make 23 more cups. Be careful not to leave any holes in the pastry or the gems will stick to the tin after they are baked. Spoon the fruit filling into the lined cups and sprinkle some of the almonds into each one of them.

Roll out the remaining dough on a lightly floured surface until it is about 3 mm (⅛ inch) thick and cut 24 rounds the same size as the tops of the gem cups. Cover each fruit gem with a round of pastry, lightly pressing on the edges of the pastry to seal them.

Bake the fruit gems until they are browned—25 to 30 minutes. Let them cool slightly. To remove the gems, cover the tin with a baking sheet or wire rack, turn both over together, and lift off the tin. Serve the fruit gems warm or at room temperature.

Fruited Phyllo Cigars

Makes 24 cigars
Working time: about 25 minutes
Total time: about 9 hours and 45 minutes (includes soaking and cooling)

Per cigar: Calories 35, Protein trace, Cholesterol 0mg,
Total fat 2g, Saturated fat 0g, Sodium 15mg

175 g/6 oz	*mixed dried fruits (peaches, pears apple rings, apricots), finely chopped*
2 tsp	*ground coriander*
1½ tbsp	*safflower oil*
2	*sheets phyllo pastry, each about 45 by 30 cm (18 by 12 inches)*
2 tbsp	*icing sugar*

Put the mixed dried fruits into a small, non-reactive saucepan; pour over about 17.5 cl (6 fl oz) of boiling water, cover the pan and leave the fruit to soak for 8 hours, or overnight.

When the fruit is plump, place the pan over a low heat and simmer the fruit, uncovered, until it is soft and the water has evaporated. Remove the pan from the heat, stir in the coriander and leave the fruit to cool.

Preheat the oven to 180°C (350°F or Mark 4).

Lightly oil a large baking sheet. Lay one sheet of phyllo on top of the other. Cut the sheets lengthwise into four equal strips, then cut each strip widthwise into three, to give a total of twenty-four 15 by 7.5 cm (6 by 3 inch) rectangles. Stack them together in one pile. Brush the top rectangle with a little oil and place a teaspoonful of the cooled fruit mixture along one of its shorter edges, leaving a 1 cm (½ inch) margin at either end of the filling. Roll up the phyllo round the fruit to form a 'cigar', then place each cigar, seam underneath, on the baking sheet. Brush the next rectangle with oil and repeat the process, continuing until all the filling and phyllo have been used.

Bake the cigars for 15 to 20 minutes, until they are crisp and golden. Transfer them to a wire rack to cool, and sift the icing sugar over them before serving.

Grated Carrot Salad

A SALAD OF GRATED RAW CARROTS MAKES A CRISP, REFRESHING HORS-
D'OEUVRE, RICH IN VITAMIN A. IT IS PARTICULARLY WELCOME IN
WINTER, WHEN MANY FRESH SALAD INGREDIENTS ARE
HARD TO COME BY.

Serves 4
Working (and total) time: about 10 minutes
Calories 30, Protein 2g, Cholesterol 0mg, Total fat 2g,
Saturated fat 1g, Sodium 15mg

60 g/2 oz	*fromage frais*
1 tbsp	*fresh lemon juice*
1/2 tsp	*grainy mustard*
2 tsp	*tarragon leaves, chopped*
250 g/8 oz	*carrots, grated in a mouli julienne or in a food processor*

In a small bowl, whisk together the *fromage frais*, lemon juice, mustard and tarragon leaves. Arrange the grated carrots in a large dish, spoon the dressing over them and serve the salad immediately.

Green Salad with Palm Hearts and Mange-Tout

Serves 12
Working (and total) time: about 30 minutes
Calories 45, Protein 2g, Cholesterol 0mg, Total fat 3g,
Saturated fat trace, Sodium 20mg

4	*little gem or other small round lettuces, cut in half, leaves washed and dried*
650 g/22 oz	*canned palm hearts, rinsed well, each cut crosswise into four equal pieces*
175 g/6 oz	*watercress sprigs, trimmed, washed and dried*
2	*cucumbers, halved lengthwise, seeded and cut mto 5 cm (2 inch) long sticks*
600 g/1 1/4 lb	*mange-tout, strings removed, blanched, refreshed under cold running water*

Lemon vinaigrette

2 tbsp	*safflower oil*
2 tbsp	*fresh lemon juice*
	freshly ground black pepper

First prepare the lemon vinaigrette. In a small bowl, mix the oil and lemon juice using a fork, and season the dressing with plenty of black pepper.

Pile all the ingredients for the salad into a large bowl. Just before serving, pour on the lemon dressing and toss the salad thoroughly.

Italian Seafood Salad

Serves 8
Working time: about 1 hour
Total time: about 4 hours (includes marinating)
Calories 120, Protein 14g, Cholesterol 100mg, Total fat
6g, Saturated fat 1g, Sodium 155mg

1¹/₂ tbsp	*virgin olive oil*
1	*onion, chopped*
500 g/1 lb	*squid, cleaned and rinsed thoroughly, pouches cut into rings, wings sliced into strips, tentacles left whole*
1	*garlic clove, crushed*
1 tbsp	*fresh lemon juice*
1 tbsp	*chopped parsley*
¹/₄ tsp	*salt*
	freshly ground black pepper
175 g/6 oz	*peeled prawns, halved lengthwise and deveined*
3	*sticks celery, thinly sliced*
250 g/8 oz	*round or other lettuce, washed, dried and shredded*
1	*red onion, thinly sliced*
2	*lemons, cut into wedges*

In a saucepan, heat ¹/₂ tablespoon of the oil, add the onion and cook it gently until it is softened, but not browned 6 to 8 minutes. Add the prepared squid and the garlic, cover the saucepan and cook gently until the squid is very tender 15 to 20 minutes. Drain the squid in a colander set over a bowl, and return the squid juices to the saucepan; boil the liquid over high heat until it is reduced by three quarters. Whisk the remaining oil, the lemon juice, parsley, salt and some freshly ground black pepper into the squid juices to make a marinade.

Put the cooked squid and the prawns into a bowl, pour the marinade over them and mix the seafood until it is well coated. Cover the mixture and place it in the refrigerator to marinate for at least 3 hours.

Just before serving, mix the sliced celery into the seafood. Serve the salad on a bed of shredded lettuce garnished with a few red onion rings, and accompanied by the lemon wedges.

EDITOR'S NOTE: If you are using baby squid in this recipe, they will cook more rapidly. Test them for tenderness after cooking for about 5 minutes.

Golden Pasta with Chanterelles

Serves 6
Working time: about 45 minutes
Total time: about 2 hours
Calories 185, Protein 6g, Cholesterol 45mg, Total fat 6g,
Saturated fat 2g, Sodium 60mg

175 g/6 oz	strong plain flour
30 g/1 oz	coarsely ground semolina
1	egg
1/4 tsp	saffron threads, pounded to a powder with a pinch of coarse salt in a mortar and dissolved in 2 tbsp of hot water
2 tsp	yellow mustard seeds
175 g/6 oz	chanterelle mushrooms

Saffron dressing

	small pinch saffron
1/8 tsp	coarse salt
3 tbsp	crème fraîche or thick soured cream
5 tbsp	fromage frais

To prepare the dough in a food processor, sift the flour and semolina into the bowl, add the egg and process the mixture until it forms fine crumbs—about 30 seconds. With the processor switched on, pour in the saffron water a little at a time and process the dough until it forms a ball. To make the pasta dough by hand, sift the flour and semolina into a bowl, make a well in the centre, and add the egg and saffron water. Slowly incorporate the flour mixture into the liquid with a fork. If the dough is sticky, add a teaspoon more flour; if crumbly, add a few drops of water. Knead the dough on a floured surface until it is very smooth and elastic about 10 minutes.

Let the dough rest for about 30 minutes—or for 1 hour if you have prepared it by hand.

To cut the pasta, divide the dough into four pieces, and roll them out thinly on a floured work surface.

Dust each rolled-out piece lightly with flour, pile up the pieces in a single neat stack, and cut the dough into very thin strips with a sharp knife or pastry cutter. Alternatively, roll out the dough and cut it into ribbons with a pasta machine. Hang the pasta over a rolling pin or a broom handle to dry for about 30 minutes.

Place the mustard seeds in a small bowl, and microwave them on high for about 2 minutes to release their aromatic oil. Remove the seeds from the microwave and crush them with a pestle.

Bring 1.25 litres (2 pints) of water to the boil in a large saucepan. Meanwhile, place the chanterelle mushrooms in a dish greased with safflower oil. Cover them with plastic film left slightly open at one side and microwave on high for 2 minutes, turning the dish half way through cooking.

To make the dressing, pound the saffron in a mortar with the salt, mix it with the crème fraîche and fromage frais, and place in the microwave on high until it is warmed through about—30 seconds.

Put the pasta in the boiling water and cook it until it is al dente—about 2 minutes. Drain thoroughly in a colander, rinse with hot water to remove all excess starch, and then drain thoroughly a second time.

Place the pasta in a large, warmed bowl. Toss it quickly with the saffron dressing, the crushed mustard seeds and the mushrooms, and serve hot.

EDITOR'S NOTE: Tiny golden oyster mushrooms may be used instead of chanterelles. To cook them, place the mushrooms in a single layer in a round dish lined with kitchen paper, cover with plastic film left slightly open at one side and microwave on high for 1 minute, turning the dish after 30 seconds. Remove the mushrooms from the microwave and leave them to rest, still on the kitchen paper, for another minute.

Leek and Bacon Potatoes

Serves 4

Working time: about 15 minutes

Total time: about 25 minutes

Calories 145, Protein 8g, Cholesterol 10mg, Total fat 2g, Saturated fat trace, Sodium 340mg

4	potatoes (about 125 g/4 oz each), scrubbed, well, dried and pricked all over with a fork
60 g/2 oz	lean smoked bacon, trimmed of fat and diced
125 g/4 oz	leeks, trimmed, cleaned and finely chopped
1 tbsp	skimmed milk
	freshly ground black pepper

Place the potatoes in a circle on a paper towel in the microwave oven. Cook the potatoes on high for 10 minutes, turning them over after 5 minutes, then remove them from the oven and set them aside.

Put the bacon and leeks into a small bowl and microwave on high for 3 minutes, stirring once.

Cut the tops off the potatoes and scoop out the insides to within 5 mm (¼ inch) of the skins. Mash the scooped out potato with the milk and season lightly with freshly ground pepper. Stir in the bacon and leeks. Pile the potato, bacon and leek mixture back into the skins, place the lids on top and reheat on high for 1 to 2 minutes before serving.

Muscat Grape Tartlets

Makes 12 tartlets
Working time: about 35 minutes
Total time: about 2 hours (includes chilling)
Per tartlet: Calories 140, Protein 3g, Cholesterol trace,
Total fat 6g, Saturated fat 2g, Sodium 70mg

275 g/9 oz	*shortcrust dough*
24	*Muscat grapes or other large firm green grapes*
4 tbsp	*thick Greek yoghurt*
	Wine syrup
15 cl/¹/₄ pint	*sweet white dessert wine*
¹/₂	*orange, rind only, cut into several pieces*
1¹/₂ tsp	*powdered gelatine*

Roll out the dough on a lightly floured surface to a thickness of 3 mm (¹/₈ inch). Using a sharp knife, cut the dough into twelve 11 by 9 cm (4¹/₂ by 3¹/₂ inch) rectangles and use these to line 12 oval tartlet tins measuring approximately 7.5 by 5 by 2 cm (3 by 2 by ¹/₄ inch). Prick the insides with a fork and chill the tartlet cases for 30 minutes. Preheat the oven to 220°C (425°F or Mark 7).

Bake the tartlet cases for 15 to 20 minutes, until the pastry is lightly browned. Remove from the oven, cool slightly and unmould on to a wire rack.

Meanwhile, prepare the wine syrup. Put the wine, sugar and orange rind into a small, non reactive saucepan and heat gently, stirring with a wooden spoon, until the sugar has dissolved. Bring the mixture almost to the boil, then remove it from the heat and allow it to stand, covered, for 30 minutes, so the syrup becomes infused with the flavour of the orange rind.

Using a slotted spoon, remove the orange rind from the syrup. Sprinkle the gelatine over 2 tablespoons of water in a small bowl and leave it to soften for 2 minutes. Set the bowl over a pan of simmering water and stir until the gelatine has fully dissolved. Whisk the warm gelatine into the wine mixture, then chill the syrup until it is beginning to set about 30 minutes.

Cut the grapes in half and remove the pips. Place 1 teaspoon of yoghurt into each pastry case, arrange four grape halves on top, then pour on a little of the wine syrup, shaking the tartlets gently to encourage the syrup to fill the spaces between grapes. Brush any remaining syrup over the surface of the grapes. Chill the tartlets for 20 to 30 minutes, until set, then serve them as soon as possible.

Moulded Asparagus Timbales

Serves 6 as a first course
Working time: about 30 minutes
Total time: about 6 hours and 30 minutes (includes chilling)
Calories 60, Protein 7g, Cholesterol 2mg, Total fat 2g, Saturated fat 1g, Sodium 110mg

500 g/1 lb	*medium asparagus, trimmed and peeled*
1/4 litre/8 fl oz	*cold unsalted chicken stock*
1 tsp	*powdered gelatine*
125 g/4 oz	*firm tofu*
100 g/3 1/2 oz	*low-fat cottage cheese*
12.5 cl/4 fl oz	*plain low fat yoghurt*
2	*spring onions, trimmed and coarsely chopped*
1	*fresh hot green chilli pepper, seeded*
3 tbsp	*finely cut fresh dill, or 1 tbsp dried dill mixed with 2 tbsp chopped parsley*
	lettuce leaves, washed and dried, for garnish

Arrange the asparagus spears in a single layer on a dinner plate. Cover the plate tightly with plastic film and microwave the asparagus on high for 2 to 3 minutes, rotating the plate a quarter turn midway through the cooking time. Set the asparagus spears aside but do not uncover them.

Pour the stock into a 60 cl (1 pint) glass measuring jug. Sprinkle the gelatine over the stock and stir it in. Microwave the mixture on high for 4 minutes, then stir it to ensure that the gelatine has dissolved. If it has not, microwave the mixture for 1 minute more.

Purée the tofu, cottage cheese, yoghurt, spring onions, chilli pepper, and dill or dill-and-parsley mixture in a food processor or blender. Pour the purée into a large bowl and stir in the gelatine mixture. Set the bowl aside.

Cut off and reserve 18 asparagus tips for garnish. Coarsely chop the remaining asparagus and combine it with the gelatine mixture. Divide the mixture evenly between six 12.5 cl (4 fl oz) ramekins. Refrigerate the ramekins until the mixture has set at—least 6 hours.

To serve, run the tip of a knife round the inside of a ramekin to loosen the sides of the timbale. Set the ramekin in a shallow bowl of hot water for 15 seconds to loosen the bottom, then invert the timbale on to a small plate. Repeat the process to unmould the other timbales. Garnish each with three asparagus tips arrange a few lettuce leaves round the timbale and serve immediately.

Pasta Salad with Tomato-Anchovy Sauce

Serves 6 as a side dish

Working time: about 1 hour and 15 minutes
Total time: about 2 hours and 15 minutes
Calories 135, Protein 4g, Cholesterol 0mg, Total fat 3g,
Saturated fat 0g, Sodium 45mg

1 tbsp	virgin olive oil
4 tbsp	finely chopped red onion
1	garlic clove, finely chopped
1/2 tsp	paprika, preferably Hungarian
1/4 tsp	cinnamon
1/4 tsp	ground cumin
	cayenne pepper
	freshly ground black pepper
750 g/1 1/2 lb	ripe tomatoes, skinned, seeded and chopped
2	anchovies, rinsed, patted dry with paper towels and cut into pieces
1 tsp	red wine vinegar
125 g/4 oz	small carrots, peeled and cut into batonnets
125 g/4 oz	French beans, trimmed and cut into 4 cm (1 1/2 inch) lengths
2	sweet yellow or red peppers
125 g/4 oz	penne or ziti
2 tbsp	chopped fresh basil

To prepare the tomato sauce, heat the oil in a large heavy frying pan over medium heat. Add the onion and garlic and sauté them, stirring frequently, until the onion is translucent—about 5 minutes. Add the paprika, cinnamon, cumin, a pinch of cayenne pepper and some black pepper; continue sautéing, stirring constantly, for 30 seconds. Stir in the tomatoes anchovy pieces, and raise the heat to medium high. Bring the sauce to a simmer and cook it, stirring frequently, until it is thickened—about 12 minutes. Remove the pan from the heat and stir in the vinegar. Set the sauce aside and let it cool thoroughly.

Meanwhile, cook the vegetables: pour enough water into a saucepan to fill it about 2.5 cm (1 inch) deep. Set a vegetable steamer in the pan and bring the water to the boil. Put the carrots and beans into the steamer, cover, and steam the vegetables until they are tender—2 to 3 minutes. Refresh them under cold running water; drain and set aside.

Roast the yellow or red peppers about 5 cm (2 inches) below a preheated grill, turning them until are blistered on all sides. Place the peppers in a bowl and cover the bowl with plastic film; the trapped steam will loosen their skins. Peel and seed the peppers, then cut them into 1 cm (1/2 inch) squares.

Add the pasta to 2 litres (3 1/2 pints) of water boiling with 1/2 teaspoon of salt. Start testing the pasta after 8 minutes and cook it until it is al dente. Drain the pasta and rinse it under cold running water, then drain it again. Transfer the pasta to a large bowl. Add the tomato sauce along with the carrots, beans, pepper pieces and basil; toss the salad well. Let the salad stand at room temperature for 1 hour before serving it.

Passion Fruit and Raspberry Roulade

Serves 6

Working time: about 40 minutes

Total time: about 1 hour and 25 minutes

Calories 225, Protein 7g, Cholesterol 80mg, Total fat 8g,
Saturated fat 2g, Sodium 155mg

4	*passion fruits*
125 g/4 oz	*thick Greek yoghurt*
3 tsp	*powdered gelatine*
1	*egg white*
30 g/1 oz	*caster sugar*
	icing sugar, for dredging
250 g/8 oz	*fresh raspberries*

Hazelnut sponge

90 g/3 oz	*shelled hazelnuts, roasted and finely ground*
45 g/1^1/2 oz	*potato flour*
2	*eggs*
90 g/3 oz	*caster sugar*
2	*egg whites*

Preheat the oven to 190°C (375°F or Mark 5). Grease a 32 by 22 cm (13 by 9 inch) Swiss roll tin, line the tin with non-stick parchment paper and grease the paper.

To make the sponge, put the hazelnuts and potato flour in a small bowl and mix them together well. Put the whole eggs and 60 g (2 oz) of the caster sugar in a large bowl, then place the bowl over a saucepan of gently simmering water, taking care that the bottom of the bowl does not touch the water. Using a hand-held electric mixer, whisk the eggs and sugar until the mixture becomes thick and pale. Remove the bowl from the heat and continue whisking until the mixture is cool and falls from the whisk in a thick ribbon trail. In a small bowl, whisk the egg whites until they are stiff, then gradually whisk into them the remaining caster sugar, until the meringue is stiff and shiny. Carefully fold the hazelnuts and flour into the whole egg mixture, then fold in the egg whites.

Pour the mixture into the prepared tin and spread it evenly. Gently tap the tin on the work surface to level the top. Bake the sponge for 15 to 20 minutes, until it is well risen, lightly browned and springy to the touch. Remove the tin from the oven and place it on a wire rack. Cover the sponge loosely with foil and leave it to cool in the tin—about 45 minutes.

Meanwhile, make the filling. Cut the passion fruits in half and spoon out their centres into a small nylon sieve set over a bowl. Press the seeds with the back of the spoon to extract the juice. Stir the Greek yoghurt into the passion fruit juice until the mixture is smooth. Put 2 tablespoons of cold water in a second small bowl; sprinkle the gelatine evenly over the surface, and set it aside. In another bowl, whisk the egg white until it will hold stiff peaks, then gradually whisk in the caster sugar until the mixture is stiff and shiny.

Set the bowl of gelatine over a saucepan of gently simmering water and stir until the gelatine has dissolved. Quickly whisk the gelatine solution into the passion fruit mixture, then gradually fold the mixture into the whisked egg white. Refrigerate the mixture until it is on the point of setting—about 10 minutes.

Lay a large sheet of non-stick parchment paper on the work surface and dredge it heavily with icing sugar. Invert the cooled sponge rectangle on to the icing sugar and remove the lining paper. Sprinkle the fresh raspberries evenly over the rectangle, then spread the passion fruit mixture evenly over the raspberries. Starting from one of the short sides, roll up the base and filling: lift one end of the underlying paper to start off the roulade, and nudge it along by gradually lifting the rest of the paper.

Wrap the roulade loosely in greaseproof paper and place it in a rigid container. Chill it until required, and serve it in a long dish; cut it into slices for serving.

EDITOR'S NOTE: To roast hazelnuts, place them on a baking sheet in a preheated 180°C (350°F or Mark 4) oven for 10 minutes, stirring them from time to time to ensure that they brown evenly. Allow the nuts to cool before grinding them.

Pastry Crescents with a Fish Filling

Makes about 40 crescents
Working time: about 1 hour
Total time: about 2 hours and 20 minutes (includes proving)
Per crescent:Calories 90, Protein 4g, Cholesterol 20mg, Total fat 4g, Saturated fat 2g, Sodium 40mg

30 g/1 oz	*fresh yeast, or 15g/¹/₂ oz dried yeast*
¹/₄ litre/8 fl oz	*skimmed milk*
75 g/2¹/₂ oz	*unsalted butter*
500 g/1 lb	*strong plain flour*
¹/₂ tsp	*salt*
1	*egg, plus a little beaten egg for brushing*
2 tbsp	*caraway seeds, for garnish*

Fish filling

¹/₂ tsp	*unsalted butter*
1	*shallot or small onion, finely chopped*
30 cl/¹/₂ pint	*unsalted fish stock*
250 g/8 oz	*herring fillet*
250 g/8 oz	*salmon or salmon trout fillet*
2 tbsp	*finely chopped fresh dill*

Cream the fresh yeast with 1 tablespoon of warm water and set aside for 10 minutes until activated; if using dried yeast, reconstitute according to the manufacturer's instructions. Warm the milk and butter in a saucepan. Sift the flour with the salt, make a well and beat in the milk and butter, yeast mixture and egg, using a wooden spoon. Turn the dough on to a floured surface, and knead until the dough feels elastic—about 10 minutes. Cover with plastic film and set aside in a warm, draught-free place until it is double its original volume—1 to 1¹/₂ hours.

Meanwhile, prepare the filling. Heat the butter in a frying pan over low heat; add the shallot and sauté gently for 10 minutes. Bring the stock to the boil in a saucepan, add the herring and salmon, and poach over low heat until the fish is just cooked through— about 3 minutes. Remove the fish from the pan with a slotted spoon, skin it and flake the flesh. Mix the fish and the dill into the shallots, and set aside to cool.

Knock back the yeast dough and knead it briefly. Divide the dough in half, and roll out the first half on a floured surface to form a rectangle approximately 40 by 28 cm (16 by 11 inches). Using a 6 cm (2¹/₂ inch) diameter round pastry cutter or the rim of an up-turned glass, cut out about 20 circles from the dough. Place a small amount of the filling in the centre of each circle; wet the edges of the circles and bring the two halves together to form a semi-circle with the filling inside. Press to seal the edges, and bend the semi-circles to form crescents. Repeat the rolling, cutting and filling procedure with the remaining dough. Trimmings can be kneaded again and used to make more crescents.

Brush the beaten egg lightly over the crescents. Sprinkle the crescents with the caraway seeds and space them apart on lightly greased baking sheets, ensuring that they do not touch. Leave them to rise while the oven heats to 200°C (400°F or Mark 6). Place the crescents in the oven and bake until golden-brown—10 to 12 minutes. Serve warm.

Pistachio and Almond
Petits Fours

THESE PETITS FOURS MAKE A DELIGHTFUL AFTER-DINNER TREAT SERVED
WITH COFFEE.

Makes 28 petits fours
Working time: about 30 minutes
Total time: about 45 minutes
Per petit four: Calories 60, Protein 1g, Cholesterol 10mg,
Total fat 4g, Saturated fat 1g, Sodium 15mg

125 g/1 oz	ground almonds
90 g/3 oz	caster sugar
30 g/1 oz	cornflour
30 g/1 oz	polyunsaturated margarine, melted and cooled
1 tbsp	soured cream
1	egg, beaten
1 tbsp	kirsch or amaretto liqueur
30 g/1 oz	shelled pistachio nuts, skinned and chopped
1 tbsp	icing sugar

Preheat the oven to 190°C (375°F or Mark 5). Have ready 28 double-thickness petits fours cases.

Mix together the almonds, caster sugar and cornflour in a mixing bowl. Make a well in the centre then pour in the margarine, soured cream, egg and kirsch or amaretto. Using a wooden spoon, blend the ingredients together until smooth.

Spoon the almond mixture into the petits fours cases, filling each one three-quarters full. Sprinkle the pistachio nuts evenly over the top of the mixture, then sift on the icing sugar.

Place the petits fours on a baking sheet and bake for 12 to 15 minutes, until risen, very lightly browned and firm to the touch. Remove from the baking sheet to a wire rack to cool.

EDITOR'S NOTE: These petits fours are best eaten on the day they are made, but they may be kept for two to three days stored in an airtight container. To skin pistachio nuts, drop them into boiling water and simmer for 1 minute, drain thoroughly, then rub them briskly in a towel.

Plantain Crisps

Serves 10

Working time: about 20 minutes
Total time: about 50 minutes
Calories 110, Protein 1g, Cholesterol 0mg, Total fat 6g,
Saturated fat 1g, Sodium trace

4 *large green plantains*
4 tbsp *safflower oil*

Top and tail the plantains with a stainless steel knife.
Slit the skin of each plantain lengthwise into quarters,
then peel off the strips of skin.

With a lightly oiled knife, slice the plantains as thinly
as possible. Place the slices in a bowl of salted water
and set aside for about 30 minutes, then drain them
and pat them dry.

Heat the oil in a non-stick frying pan over medium
heat and fry the first batch of plantain slices for 1½ to
2 minutes, turning once, until they are golden-brown.
Cook the remaining slices in the same way. As each
batch is cooked, remove the slices from the pan with
a slotted spoon and lay them on paper towels to ab-
sorb any excess fat. Serve the plantain crisps hot, in a
lined basket or on a large plate.

Salad of Lettuce and Nasturtium Flowers

Serves 6

Working (and total) time: about 20 minutes
Calories 25, Protein 1g, Cholesterol 10mg, Total fat 2g,
Saturated fat 1g, Sodium 75mg

1 *small cos lettuce, or two little gem*
  lettuces, leaves washed and dried
1 *red lollo lettuce, leaves washed and dried*
12 *nasturtium flowers*
Mustard-lemon dressing
4 tbsp *soured cream*
2 tbsp *fresh lemon juice*
2 tsp *Dijon mustard*
¼ tsp *salt*
  freshly ground black pepper
2 tbsp *finely cut chives*

Tear or cut the lettuce leaves into pieces and put
them into a lidded plastic container. Place the nasturtium flowers in a separate rigid container. Refrigerate
both until you are ready to go to the picnic.

To make the dressing, put all the ingredients into a
screw-top jar and shake them together vigorously.
Chill the dressing until it is required.

Before serving, shake the dressing again, then pour
it into the bottom of a serving bowl. Place the salad
leaves in the bowl and arrange the flowers on top.
Just before serving, toss the salad with the dressing.

Salad of Leaves and Flowers

EDIBLE FLOWERS, SUCH AS VIOLETS, ROSE PETALS AND NASTURTIUM
LEAVES, ADD COLOUR AND PIQUANCY TO SIMPLE TOSSED SALADS.
SOME GREENGROCERS AND SUPERMARKETS NOW STOCK A VARIETY OF
EDIBLE BLOOMS. IF YOU ARE USING GARDEN FLOWERS AVOID ANY THAT
HAVE BEEN SPRAYED WITH CHEMICALS AND INSECTICIDES. FLOWERS
SOLD BY FLORISTS SHOULD **NOT** BE USED FOR CULINARY PURPOSES.

Serves 6

Working (and total) time: about 10 minutes

Calories 75, Protein 1g, Cholesterol 0mg, Total fat 8g,
Saturated fat 1g, Sodium 5mg

1	lettuce heart, separated into leaves, washed and dried
5	oak leaf lettuce leaves, washed and dried
30 g/1 oz	curly endive, washed and dried
8	nasturtium leaves
2 tsp	lavender florets
1 tsp	borage flowers
2 tsp	thyme flowers
8	rose petals
6	violets or pansies
6	chervil sprigs

Tarragon vinaigrette

3 tbsp	safflower oil
1¹/₂ tbsp	white wine vinegar
1 tsp	crushed coriander seeds
	freshly ground black pepper
¹/₂ tsp	fresh tarragon leaves

In a small bowl, whisk together the oil and the vinegar
for the dressing. Stir in the coriander seeds, some
pepper and the tarragon, and mix well.

Lay the lettuce, the endive and the nasturtium
leaves loosely in a deep bowl. Sprinkle the lavender,
borage and thyme flowers, the rose petals, the violets or pansies and the chervil over the top. Add the
dressing, toss the salad and serve it immediately.

EDITOR'S NOTE: Any selection of mild and bitter salad
leaves and edible flowers can be used. Aim for a combi-
nation that offers vivid contrasts of colour, flavour and
texture. Perfect freshness of all ingredients is the sole
requirement.

Salmon-Filled Choux Buns

CHOUX DOUGH IS MORE COMMONLY USED FOR SWEET PASTRIES SUCH
AS ÉCLAIRS OR PROFITEROLES. HERE IT FORMS THE BASIS OF AN
ELEGANT, BUT SIMPLE, HORS-D'OEUVRE.

Serves 6

Working (and total) time: about 1 hour and 30 minutes
Calories 225, Protein 12g, Cholesterol 90mg, Total fat
13g, saturated fat 4g, Sodium 295mg

60 cl/1 pint	*unsalted fish stock*
15 cl/¼ pint	*dry white wine*
⅛ tsp	*salt*
	freshly ground black pepper
½	*small lemon, juice only*
175 g/6 oz	*salmon tail, skinned, filleted and cut into six equal portions*
175 g/6 oz	*fine French beans*
15 g/½ oz	*polyunsaturated margarine, chilled and cut into small cubes*

Choux dough

45 g/1½ oz	*polyunsaturated margarine*
75 g/½ oz	*plain flour, sifted*
2	*eggs, beaten*
30 g/1 oz	*smoked salmon, finely chopped*
1 tbsp	*finely chopped fresh dill or fennel leaves*

Preheat the oven to 200°C (400°F or Mark 6). To
make the choux dough, put the margarine in a small
saucepan with 12.5 cl (4 fl oz) of water, and cook over
medium heat just until the liquid comes to the boil.
Remove the pan from the heat and quickly beat in the
flour, all at once. Continue beating until the mixture
holds together and is free of lumps. Return the pan to
a low heat and cook the dough gently for about 1
minute to dry it out a little.

Remove the pan from the heat and add the beaten
eggs, a little at a time, beating well after each addition. Stir in the smoked salmon and the dill or fennel
leaves.

Grease a baking sheet and spoon the choux mixture on to the sheet, forming six small piles. Place the
choux buns in the oven and bake them until they are
well risen and golden all over—about 25 to 30 minutes. Meanwhile, prepare a sauce for the beans.

In a saucepan, combine 45 cl (¾ pint) of the fish
stock with the white wine and boil the mixture over
high heat to reduce it by two thirds of its volume. Season the mixture with the salt and some pepper, stir in
the lemon juice, and set the sauce aside.

When the choux buns are cooked, slit them horizontally to form six lids and six bases. Turn the oven
down to its lowest setting and return the lids and
bases to the oven to dry out slightly.

Meanwhile, poach the salmon fillet pieces in the
remaining 15 cl (¼ pint) of fish stock until they turn
pale pink—3 to 5 minutes.

Fill a saucepan with a large quantity of boiling water, plunge in the French beans and boil them until
they are cooked but still crunchy—2 to 5 minutes. Set
them aside and keep them warm.

Reheat the fish stock and wine mixture over gentle
heat and whisk in the cold margarine cubes to thicken
it. Keep the sauce warm while you fill the buns.

Place one portion of the poached salmon fillet in
each choux bun and set the pastry lid on top. Toss the
French beans in the sauce and serve them alongside
the filled buns.

Scallop Galettes

Serves 8

Working time: about 45 minutes
Total time about 1 hour
Calories 165, Protein 9g, Cholesterol 50mg, Total fat 6g,
Saturated fat 3g, Sodium 270mg

100 g/3½ oz	buckwheat flour
45 g/1½ oz	plain flour
¼ tsp	salt
30 g/1 oz	unsalted butter
1 tsp	clear honey
1	egg, lightly beaten
22. 5 cl/7½ fl oz	dry cider
500 g/1 lb	spinach, washed, stems removed
45 g/1½ oz	creme fraiche
	freshly ground black pepper
	grated nutmeg
¼ tsp	safflower oil
8	shelled scallops, bright white connective tissue removed, scallops rinsed, corals reserved freshly ground green peppercorns (optional)

To make the galette batter, first sift the flours and ¼ teaspoon of the salt into a mixing bowl and form a well in the centre. Melt 15 g (½ oz) of the butter and pour it into the well with ½ teaspoon of the honey, the egg, 15 cl (¼ pint) of the cider and 15 cl (¼ pint) of water. Using a wooden spoon, gradually draw the dry ingredients into the liquids. Beat lightly until free of lumps, then set aside to rest for about 30 minutes.

Place the washed spinach, with water still clinging to the leaves, in a large, heavy-bottomed saucepan. Cover, and steam the spinach over medium heat until wilted—2 to 3 minutes. Drain the spinach quickly squeeze out all excess moisture and chop roughly with a knife. Return the spinach to the saucepan and stir in 1 tablespoon of the remaining cider and half the créme fraîche. Season with ¼ teaspoon of the salt and some pepper and nutmeg. Set aside until you are ready to serve the galettes.

When the batter is ready, heat an 18 cm (7 inch) crêpe or non-stick frying pan over medium-high heat. Add the oil and spread it over the entire surface with a paper towel. Put 2 to 3 tablespoons of the batter into the pan, and immediately swirl the pan to coat the bottom with a thin, even layer of batter. Cook until the bottom is lightly browned—about 30 seconds. Lift the edge with a spatula and turn the galettes over. Cook it on the second side until that too is lightly browned. Slide the galette on to a heated plate.

Repeat the process with the remaining batter, brushing the pan lightly with more oil if the galettes begin to stick. Stack the cooked galettes on the plate as you go, and then cover with a tea towel and set aside; or keep them warm in a 150°C (300°F or Mark 2) oven until all eight are cooked and ready to fill.

Slice each scallop horizontally into two or three rounds. Finely slice the corals. Melt the remaining butter in a heavy frying pan and toss the scallop slices in the butter until they are no longer opaque—about 2 minutes. Add the remaining cider and the sliced corals, and cook over medium heat for a furthe seconds. Mix in the rest of the créme fraîche, honey and salt, season with some nutmeg and return to the heat for a few seconds to amalgamate. Remove the frying pan from the heat. Reheat the spinach mixture over medium heat, stirring continuously.

To serve, place a spoonful of spinach in the centre of each galette and arrange two or three scallop slices and a sprinkling of coral in each 'nest' of spinach. Fold over the four rounded edges of each galette to form a small, square parcel, leaving the scallop slices partly exposed. Sprinkle a little freshly ground green pepper over the top of each scallop filling if you like, and serve immediately.

Scallop and Lime Choux Puffs

Makes 16 puffs
Working time: about 40 minutes
Total time: about 1 hour and 20 minutes
Per puff: Calories 80, Protein 6g, Cholesterol 45mg, Total
fat 4g, Saturated fat 2g, Sodium 105mg

350 g/12 oz	*raw scallops, bright white connective tissue removed, rinsed and cut into 5 mm (¹/₄ inch) dice*
1¹/₂ tsp	*cornflour*
1¹/₂ tbsp	*fresh lime juice*
¹/₄ tsp	*grated lime rind*
1¹/₂ tbsp	*finely chopped parsley*
¹/₄ tsp	*salt*
	freshly ground black pepper
60 g/2 oz	*fromage frais*

Choux dough

60 g/2 oz	*unsalted butter*
¹/₄ tsp	*salt*
75 g/2¹/₂ oz	*plain flour*

To make the choux dough, place the butter and salt in a small heavy-bottomed saucepan containing 15 cl (¹/₄ pint) of water, and heat to boiling point. Add all the flour, and beat the mixture until it comes away cleanly from the pan sides. Remove the pan from the heat.

Beat the eggs with a little cayenne pepper, then add them to the dough; beat until the eggs are absorbed and a stiff, glossy paste is formed.

Preheat the oven to 230°C (450°F or Mark 8).

Lightly oil a baking sheet. Fit a piping bag with a 2 cm (³/₄ inch) plain nozzle, fill it with choux dough and pipe 16 walnut-sized rounds on to the baking sheet. Cook the choux rounds in the oven for 10 minutes, then reduce the heat to 180°C (350°F or Mark 4) and cook for a further 25 to 30 minutes until the puffs are well risen and golden.

Slice through each choux puff about a third of the way from the top to allow the steam to escape, and leave to cool on a wire rack until required.

For the filling, sprinkle the scallops with the cornflour, turning and mixing to coat them evenly. Heat a dry, non-stick pan over high heat, add the scallops and, stirring all the time, sear them until they begin to colour—about 1 minute. Reduce the heat, add the lime juice and rind, parsley, salt, some pepper and the *fromage frais* to the pan, and continue to cook, stirring, until the juices thicken—about 2 minutes.

Warm the choux puffs through in a 180°C (350°F or Mark 4) oven. Spoon the scallop filling into the puffs and serve immediately.

EDITOR'S NOTE: The choux puffs may be prepared in advance and stored in an airtight container for up to five days before being warmed through and filled. Alternatively, they can be frozen, and thawed in the oven as they are needed.

Seafood Canapés

Makes 12 canapés
Working time: about 1 hour
Total time: about 2 hours and 30 minutes (includes
cooling and setting)
Per canape: Calories 40, Protein 2g, Cholesterol 30mg,
Total fat 2g, Saturated fat trace, Sodium 110mg

175 g/6 oz	*haddock fillet*
1	*egg white*
$^3/_8$ tsp	*salt*
90 g/3 oz	*thick Greek yoghurt*
	freshly ground black pepper
3 or 4	*thin slices wholemeal bread, toasted*
15 g/$^1/_2$ oz	*polyunsaturated margarine*
$^1/_2$ tsp	*tomato paste*
2 tsp	*finely chopped basil leaves*
15 cl/$^1/_4$ pint	*vegetable aspic, melted*
12	*peeled cooked prawns*
3 tsp	*black caviare or lump fish roe*

Rinse the haddock fillet under cold running water and pat it dry with paper towels. Carefully remove the skin from the haddock, then remove any bones and cut the fish roughly into cubes. Put the haddock into a food processor or blender with the egg white and $^1/_4$ tsp of the salt, and blend to a smooth paste. Work the paste through a nylon sieve into a bowl to remove any coarse sinews. Cover the bowl and refrigerate the mixture for 30 minutes.

Meanwhile, grease 12 tiny, differently shaped moulds. Pour enough water into a saucepan to fill it about 2.5 cm (1 inch) deep, set a steamer in the pan and bring the water to the boil.

Remove the chilled fish mixture from the refrigerator. Gradually beat in the yoghurt, and season with some black pepper. Fill the prepared moulds with the fish mousse. Place the moulds in the steamer and cover them closely with a sheet of non-stick parchment paper; steam until the mousse is firm—1$^1/_2$ to 2 minutes. Remove the moulds from the steamer and refrigerate until quite cold.

Using a 4 cm (1$^3/_4$ inch) plain round cutter, cut 12 rounds from the toast. Put the margarine, tomato paste, basil, the remaining salt and a little pepper into a bowl, and beat together until smooth. Spread the mixture thinly over each round of toast.

Carefully unmould the haddock mousses. Dip each mousse, balanced on a fork, in the vegetable aspic and place it on a round of toast. Put the canapés on a wire rack over a tray, and refrigerate them for about 5 minutes to set the aspic. Dip the peeled prawns in the aspic and place one prawn neatly on each canapé. Refrigerate for 5 minutes to set the aspic.

Stir the remaining aspic over ice, or refrigerate, until it begins to thicken. Carefully spoon the aspic over the canapés to coat them evenly. Immediately, spoon little caviare on to each one. Refrigerate for about 2 minutes to set firmly. Keep the canapés refrigerate until just before serving.

EDITOR'S NOTE: The haddock mousses may be made the day before and kept in the refrigerator.

Sesame-Prawn Toasts

Makes 48 toasts
Working time: about 45 minutes
Total time: about 1 hour

Per toast: Calories 15, Protein 1g, Cholesterol 5mg, Total fat trace, Saturated fat trace, Sodium 25mg

1 tsp	*fresh lemon juice*
125 g/4 oz	*cooked peeled prawns, finely chopped*
175 g/6 oz	*lemon sole fillets, or other white-fleshed fish*
2 tsp	*dry vermouth*
1	*egg white*
1/4 tsp	*salt*
3 tbsp	*fromage frais*
3 tbsp	*finely chopped spring onions*
	cayenne pepper
6	*thin slices white bread, trimmed to 9 cm (3 1/2 inch) squares*
4 tsp	*white sesame seeds*
	lettuce leaves, for garnish

Add the lemon juice to the chopped prawns and set the mixture aside. In a food processor, purée the fish fillets with the vermouth, egg white and salt. Transfer the mixture from the processor to a bowl and set this in a larger bowl containing ice. Beat in the *fromage frais*, then gently stir in the chopped spring onions, cayenne pepper and chopped prawns. Meanwhile, preheat the oven to 200°C (400°F or Mark 6).

Toast the bread under the grill until lightly browned. Spread the prawn topping over the toast and cover with an even sprinkling of sesame seeds. Cut the toast slices into quarters, then cut each quarter diagonally into two triangles. Place the triangles on a baking sheet and bake them in the oven until they are golden-brown—15 to 20 minutes. Serve the sesame-prawn toasts warm on a bed of salad leaves.

Sole and Asparagus Tartlets

Serves 6

Working time: about 1 hour

Total time: about 3 hours (includes chilling)

Calories 240, Protein 12g, Cholesterol 50mg, Total fat
13g, Saturated fat 3g, Sodium 260mg

175 g/6 oz	*skinned sole fillets*
1	*egg white*
150 g/5 oz	*plus 2 tbsp thick Greek yoghurt*
1/4 tsp	*salt*
	freshly ground black pepper
250 g/8 oz	*asparagus, trimmed, peeled and thinly sliced*
45 g/1 1/2 oz	*smoked salmon, cut into fine strips*
2 tsp	*finely cut chives*
	thinly sliced cucumber, for garnish

Tartlet shells

125 g/4 oz	*plain flour*
1/8 tsp	*salt*
60 g/2 oz	*polyunsaturated margarine*
1	*egg yolk*

To prepare the filling, place the sole fillets and egg white in a food processor and process them until they form a smooth paste. Set a nylon sieve over a bowl, and work the paste through the sieve to remove any coarse fibres. Cover the bowl with plastic film and refrigerate the sole and egg mixture while you prepare the tartlet shells.

To make the pastry, sift the flour and salt into a mixing bowl. Rub the margarine into the flour until the mixture resembles fine breadcrumbs; make a well in the centre. Pour the egg yolk and 1 tablespoon of water into the well and mix the ingredients, using a table knife or your hands, until a firm dough is formed.

Knead the dough on a lightly floured surface, then roll the dough out thinly. Cut out six rounds of dough measuring about 12.5 cm (5 inches) in diameter. Line six 10 cm (4 inch) fluted tartlet tins with the dough, pressing it well into the flutes and trimming the edges. Prick the pastry lightly with a fork, and refrigerate it for 30 minutes. Meanwhile, preheat the oven to 220°C (425°F or Mark 7).

Remove the chilled sole from the refrigerator. Gradually beat in 12.5 cl (4 fl oz) of the yoghurt, the salt and some pepper. Cover the fish mixture with plastic film and return it to the refrigerator.

Bring a saucepan of water to the boil and cook the sliced asparagus until it is tender—1 to 2 minutes. Pour the asparagus into a colander, refresh it under cold running water and drain it well.

Place the chilled pastry shells on a baking sheet and bake them for 10 minutes. Remove them from the oven and reduce the oven temperature to 180°C (350°F or Mark 4). Divide the asparagus equally among the pastry cases, arranging the pieces neatly in the bottom of each one. Spoon the sole mixture on top of the asparagus, spreading it evenly. Return the tartlets to the oven and cook them until the sole mixture is very lightly set—6 to 8 minutes.

Remove the tartlets from the oven and set them aside to cool. When they are cold enough to handle, carefully lift them from their tins, place them on a tray and cover with foil. Refrigerate the tartlets until they are well chilled—about 2 hours.

Just before serving, spread the remaining yoghurt in a thin layer evenly over the top of each tartlet, arrange strips of smoked salmon around its edges, and sprinkle with the chives.

Serve the tartlets on individual plates, garnished with thinly sliced cucumber.

Shredded Beef Salad with Marinated Carrot Strips

Serves 8 as a main course
Working time: about 45 minutes
Total time: about 4 hours
Calories 255, Protein 27g, Cholesterol 75mg, Total fat
12g, Saturated fat 4g, Sodium 190mg

3 tbsp	*safflower oil*
1 kg/2 lb	*lean beef chuck, or other braising steak, trimmed of fat*
6	*medium carrots*
1/4 litre/8 fl oz	*unsalted veal or chicken stock*
2	*onions, coarsely chopped*
3	*garlic cloves, crushed*
1 tbsp	*fresh thyme, or 1 tsp dried thyme*
3	*bay leaves*
1 tsp	*sugar*
12.5 cl/4 floz	*cider vinegar*
1/4 tsp	*salt*
2 tbsp	*hoisin sauce*
	freshly ground black pepper
	several Chinese cabbage or Batavian endive leaves, washed and dried
4	*spring onions (optional), cut into brushes and soaked in iced water*

Heat 1 tablespoon of the safflower oil in a large, heavy sauté pan over medium-high heat. Add the beef and sear it in the oil until it is well browned on all sides— about 10 minutes.

Slice one of the carrots into thin rounds and add it to the pan along with the stock, onions, garlic, thyme and bay leaves. Pour in enough water to raise the depth of the liquid in the pan to about 2.5 cm (1 inch). Bring the liquid to a simmer, then reduce the heat to low; partially cover the pan and cook the beef slowly until it is quite tender—about 3 hours. If the liquid falls below 5 mm (1/4 inch) during the cooking, add another 12.5 cl (4 fl oz) of water to the pan.

While the meat is cooking, use a vegetable peeler to pare long, thin strips from the outside of the remaining five carrots; discard the woody cores. Put the strips into a large bowl with the sugar and all but 2 tablespoons of the vinegar; toss well. Set the carrot strips aside to marinate, stirring them from time to time.

When the beef is tender, remove it from the pan and set it aside. Strain the cooking liquid; pour half of it into a small saucepan and discard the rest. Rapidly boil the liquid until only 4 tablespoons remain. Skim any fat from the surface and set the liquid aside.

When the beef is cool enough to handle, shred it with your fingers, discarding any fat. Heat 1 tablespoon of the remaining oil in the pan over medium-high heat. Add the beef and the salt; sauté the beef, stirring constantly, for 1 minute. Pour in the reduced cooking liquid, the remaining vinegar and the hoisin sauce; sprinkle in some pepper and cook the beef for 1 minute more, stirring all the while. Transfer the beef to a bowl and chill it.

Rinse out and dry the sauté pan, then return it to the stove over medium-high heat. Pour in the remaining oil; when it is hot, add the carrot strips and their marinade. Sauté the strips, stirring constantly, until all the liquid has evaporated—1 to 2 minutes. Transfer the carrot strips to a bowl and chill them for 30 minutes.

To serve the salad, arrange the Chinese cabbage or Batavian endive leaves on a large plate; scatter the carrot strips on top, mound the beef in the centre and garnish with the spring onions if you are using them.

Spinach and Salmon Canapés

Makes 12 canapés
Working time: about 25 minutes
Total time: about 30 minutes
Per canapé: Calories 90, Protein 9g, Cholesterol 25mg,
Total fat 4g, Saturated fat 1g, Sodium 140mg

250 g/8 oz	salmon steak, skinned and boned
2	egg whites
175 g/6 oz	skinned sole or plaice fillets
2 tbsp	quark
1	small sweet red pepper, pricked all over with a fork
175 g/6 oz	spinach leaves, stemmed, washed and drained
6	slices wholemeal bread

Finely chop the salmon in a food processor, then blend in one egg white. Tip the mixture into a bowl. Repeat this procedure with the sole or plaice and the second egg white. Stir 1 tablespoon of the quark into each of the mixtures and chill them.

Place the red pepper on a paper towel in the microwave oven and microwave on high for 4 minutes, turning after every minute. Put the pepper in a small bowl, cover with plastic film and leave to cool. Peel off the skin and remove the seeds, then cut out 12 small diamond shapes from the flesh. Set aside.

Put the spinach leaves in a bowl, cover and microwave on high for 4 minutes. Drain the spinach well, taking care not to break up the leaves.

Line the hollows of two plastic egg cartons with plastic film. Divide the sole mixture equally among the 12 moulds and smooth the surface. Divide the spinach leaves into 12 portions and arrange each portion in an even layer over the sole. Top the spinach with an even layer of the salmon mixture. Cook one box at a time on high for 1½ to 2 minutes, until the fish mixtures are just firm to the touch.

Meanwhile, toast the bread and cut out 12 circles with a 4.5 cm (1¾ inch) round cutter.

Put a plate over each carton and invert it to remove the fish moulds; drain off any liquid. Lift each mould on to a circle of toast and place a red pepper diamond on top. Arrange the assembled canapés on a plate and serve them warm.

EDITOR'S NOTE: If you wish to serve the canapés cold, let the fish moulds cool in the egg cartons, then place them on the circles of toast just before serving. Small egg cups may be used in place of plastic egg cartons to cook the fish moulds. The unused sweet pepper may be sliced and used in a salad or puréed for a sauce.

Tabbouleh

Serves 6
Working time: about 30 minutes
Total time: about 1 hour (includes soaking)
Calories 75, Protein 3g, Cholesterol 0mg, Total fat 3g,
Saturated fat 1g, Sodium 10mg

90 g/3 oz *burghul*
20 g/³/₄ oz *mint leaves, finely chopped*
60 g/2 oz *parsley, finely chopped*
1 *onion, finely chopped*
3 tbsp *fresh lemon juice*
1 tbsp *virgin olive oil*
tomato wedges, for garnish

Put the burghul in a bowl and add sufficient boiling water to cover it. Leave the burghul to soak for 30 minutes, topping up the water as necessary to keep the grains covered. Tip the burghul into a nylon sieve and let it drain thoroughly; press it down with the back of a spoon to force out as much moisture as possible.

Turn the drained burghul into a mixing bowl and add the mint, parsley, onion, lemon juice and oil. Stir all the ingredients together thoroughly. Turn the tabbouleh into a lidded plastic container to take to the picnic, and place it in the refrigerator until required. Chill the tomato wedges in a separate container.

At the picnic, transfer the tabbouleh to a serving bowl and garnish it with the tomato wedges.

Two-Potato Salad

Serves 12
Working time: about 30 minutes
Total time: about 1 hour and 15 minutes
Calories 80, Protein 2g, Cholesterol 0mg, Total fat trace,
Saturated fat trace, Sodium 35mg

500 g/1 lb *sweet potatoes, scrubbed*
500 g/1 lb *new potatoes, scrubbed, halved if large*
250 g/8 oz *spring onions, trimmed and cut diagonally into thirds*
2 tsp *Dijon mustard*
15 cl/¹/₄ pint *plain low-fat yoghurt*
white pepper
2 tbsp *capers, rinsed well, dried and roughly chopped*

Place the sweet potatoes and new potatoes into separate heavy-bottomed saucepans and pour in sufficient cold water to cover the potatoes in each pan by 2.5 cm (1 inch). Bring both pans to the boil, then reduce the heat and simmer the vegetables until they are tender—15 to 20 minutes for the new potatoes, and 25 to 30 minutes for the sweet potatoes.

Drain the potatoes and set them aside, on separate plates, until they are cool enough to handle. Peel the sweet potatoes and cut them into slices. Arrange the slices in a serving dish with the new potatoes and the spring onion pieces.

In a small bowl, stir the Dijon mustard into the yoghurt and season with some white pepper. Pour this dressing over the potatoes and onions, and sprinkle the capers over the top of the salad.

Turkish Beef and Pine-Nut Rolls

Serves 12

Working time: about 30 minutes
Total time: about 45 minutes
Calories 115, Protein 8g, Cholesterol 20mg, Total fat 6g,
Saturated fat 2g, Sodium 70mg

1 tbsp	virgin olive oil
1	onion, finely chopped
250 g/8 oz	lean minced beef
1 tsp	ground cumin
¹/₂ tsp	ground allspice
2 tbsp	pine-nuts
¹/₄ tsp	salt
2 tbsp	chopped parsley
	freshly ground black pepper
9	sheets phyllo pastry, each 30 cm (12 inches)square
30 g/1 oz	unsalted butter, melted

Heat the oil in a heavy frying pan and fry the onion until it is soft. Add the beef and fry it until it has lost its red colour, then add the cumin and allspice and fry for another minute. Stir in the pine-nuts, salt, parsley, some pepper and 2 tablespoons of water, and cook the mixture for about 10 minutes. Remove it from the heat and set it aside to cool slightly while you prepare the phyllo pastry.

Preheat the oven to 190°C (375°F or Mark 5). Cut the phyllo pastry into 7.5 cm (3 inch) wide strips and use the beef mixture to make up the rolls as demonstrated below, covering the phyllo you are not working on with a dampened tea towel to prevent it from drying out and becoming brittle.

Place the phyllo rolls on a baking sheet, brush them with the remaining butter, and bake them until they are golden-brown and crisp—about 15 minutes. Serve them immediately.

Perfect Packages from Phyllo Pastry

1 PREPARING THE PASTRY. Place a teaspoon of filling on the top strip of phyllo pastry 2.5 cm (1 inch) from the end. Starting from the opposite end, lightly brush three quarters of the pastry strip with melted butter.

2 FORMING THE ROLLS. Working from the unbuttered end, fold the pastry over the filling and roll up to the buttered section. Before continuing the roll, fold the sides of the pastry over the filling to seal the ends. Continue to roll the cylinder to the end of the pastry strip. Turn the cylinder over so that the seam is underneath.

Vegetable Wholemeal Pizza

Serves 4

Working time: about 25 minutes

Total time: about 45 minutes

Calories 250, Protein 12g, Cholesterol 10mg, Total fat 9g,
Saturated fat 3g, Sodium 420mg

1/4 tsp	*dried yeast*
175 g/6 oz	*wholemeal flour*
1/4 tsp	*salt*
15 g/1/2 oz	*polyunsaturated margarine*
3	*tomatoes, quartered*
1	*small onion, chopped*
1 tsp	*virgin olive oil*
	freshly ground black pepper
1	*courgette, sliced*
5	*sweet red pepper rings*
4	*baby sweetcorn*
60 g/2 oz	*mushrooms, sliced*
1 tsp	*dried oregano*
60 g/2 oz	*low-fat mozzarella, grated*

Reconstitute the dried yeast according to the manufacturer's instructions. Sift the flour and 1/8 teaspoon of the salt into a mixing bowl, adding back the bran from the sieve. Rub in the margarine, then make a well in the centre; pour the yeast into the well and mix it in with a wooden spoon to make a dough that can be formed into a ball.

Turn out the dough on to a lightly floured surface and knead until it is smooth and elastic—5 to 10 minutes. To prove the dough, put it in a bowl, cover with plastic film and microwave on high for 10 seconds only. Leave to stand for 10 minutes, then microwave on high for a further 10 seconds and leave to rise for 10 minutes; it should double in bulk.

Meanwhile, cook the vegetables. Place the tomatoes on a plate. Microwave on high for 1 to 2 minutes, then remove the skins and chop the flesh. Put the onion in a small bowl with 1/2 teaspoon of the oil and microwave on high for 2 minutes. Add the tomatoes and season lightly with the remaining salt and a little pepper. Set aside.

Put the courgette, pepper rings, baby sweetcorn and mushrooms in a small bowl with 1 tablespoon of water; cover with plastic film, leaving one corner open, and cook on high for 3 minutes. Drain the vegetables.

Turn the dough out on to a floured surface and knead lightly for 1 minute, then roll it out into a 25 cm (10 inch) circle. Lightly brush a flat 25 cm (10 inch) diameter plate with the remaining oil and place the dough on the plate. Spread the tomato and onion mixture over the dough and arrange the other vegetables over the top of the tomatoes. Sprinkle the oregano and grated mozzarella over the vegetables. Prove the pizza by microwaving it on high for 10 seconds, then resting it for 5 minutes. Cook on high for 5 to 6 minutes. Rest for a further 5 minutes before serving.

Vegetable Aspic

To make a clear vegetable aspic, the bowls and cooking utensils must be scrupulously clean. Here, everything is scalded to ensure that the liquid does not become clouded by impurities.

Makes about 90 cl (1¹/₂ pints)
Working time: about 45 minutes
Total time: about 2 hours and 45 minutes
Per total recipe: Calories 410, Protein 53g, Cholesterol 0mg, Total fat trace, Saturated fat 0g, Sodium 480mg

250 g/8 oz	*carrots, sliced*
250 g/8 oz	*leeks, sliced*
2	*onions, finely chopped*
4	*sticks celery, sliced*
1	*small bunch parsley*
1	*rosemary sprig*
1	*thyme sprig*
4	*garlic cloves, unpeeled*
¹/₂ tsp	*salt*
8	*black peppercorns*
45 g/1¹/₂ oz	*powdered gelatine*
2	*eggs, whites only, washed shells reserved*
1 tbsp	*red wine vinegar*

Put the carrots, leeks, onions, celery, parsley, rosemary, thyme, garlic, salt and peppercorns into a large saucepan with 1.75 litres (3 pints) of cold water. Bring to the boil, then reduce the heat and partially cover the saucepan with a lid. Simmer gently for about 2 hours, or until the liquid is reduced by half.

Strain the stock through a nylon sieve into a large bowl; discard the vegetables. Measure the stock, and make up to 90 cl (1¹/₂ pints) with water, if necessary.

Rinse the saucepan and fill it with cold water. Put a wire whisk, a large metal sieve and a large square of muslin into the saucepan. Bring the water to the boil. Remove the whisk, sieve and muslin from the pan; pour the boiling water into a large bowl to scald it, then pour the water away. Place the sieve over the bowl and line the sieve with the muslin.

Pour the stock back into the saucepan and add the gelatine, egg whites and shells, and vinegar. With the scalded whisk, whisk the stock over moderate heat until the egg whites form a thick foam on the surface.

Stop whisking, then bring the mixture to the boil sothat the foam rises to the top of the saucepan—do not allow it to boil over. Remove the saucepan from the heat and allow the foam to settle back down. Repeat this process twice more, then allow the mixture to stand for 5 minutes.

Very gently and carefully pour the aspic through the lined sieve, without allowing the foam floating on top of the liquid to break up. Leave to drain thoroughly, then let the aspic cool. Once it has cooled, the aspic sets to a jelly-like consistency.

Vegetable aspic may be kept in the refrigerator for a few days, ready to be used when needed. Once set, it can be quickly melted again by placing the bowl over a saucepan of hot water.

Turkish Delight

Serves 6

Working time: about 20 minutes

Total time: about 3 hours and 35 minutes

Calories 70, Protein 3g, Cholesterol 0mg, Total fat 3g,
Saturated fat 2g, Sodium 5mg

1/2 litre/16 fl oz	*unsweetened white grapejuice*
15 g/1/2 oz	*shelled walnuts*
15 g/1/2 oz	*powdered gelatine*
1/2 tbsp	*orange-flower water*
1/2 tsp	*pure vanilla extract*
	walnut oil, for brushing
15 g/1/2 oz	*desiccated coconut*

Preheat the oven to 180°C (350°F or Mark 4).

Pour the unsweetened grape juice into a wide, heavy-bottomed saucepan and boil it gently until it has reduced to 1/4 litre (8 fl oz). Transfer the grape juice to a bowl and set it aside.

Spread out the walnuts on a baking sheet and roast them in the oven for 15 minutes, stirring them occasionally during this time. When they are cool enough to handle, chop them roughly.

Sprinkle the gelatine over 5 tablespoons of cold water in a small, heatproof bowl. Leave the gelatine for 2 minutes, to allow the granules to soften and swell, then set the bowl over a pan of gently simmering water and stir until the gelatine has completely dissolved— about 3 minutes. Stir the gelatine solution, the orange-flower water and the vanilla extract into the reduced grape juice. Chill the mixture until it is on the point of setting—about 15 minutes.

Brush a 10 by 10 by 2.5 cm (4 by 4 by 1 inch) square tin or rigid plastic container with a little walnut oil. Stir the chopped walnuts into the partially set grape jelly, then turn the mixture into the prepared tin. Chill the grape jelly until it has set—at least 3 hours, or preferably overnight.

Unmould the set jelly on to a wooden board and cut it into 12 equal squares. Dip the squares in the desiccated coconut, pressing it on gently to ensure that each square is evenly coated. Store the squares in the refrigerator, until shortly before you serve.

Tossed Salad with Eggs and French Beans

Serves 6
Working time: about 15 minutes
Total time: about 40 minutes (includes marinating)
Calories 115, Protein 3g, Cholesterol 75mg Total fat 10g,
Saturated fat 2g Sodium 100mg

1/2	*small red onion, cut thinly into rings*
1	*small red lollo lettuce, washed and dried, leaves torn*
30 g/1 oz	*rocket, washed and dried*
90 g/3 oz	*French beans, topped and blanched for 3 minutes in boiling water*
2	*eggs, hard-boiled, each cut into six wedges*
6	*black olives*
3	*red basil sprigs*
3	*green basil sprigs*
	Vinaigrette dressing
1	*garlic clove, crushed*
1/4 tsp	*salt*
	freshly ground black pepper
1 tbsp	*red wine vinegar*
3 tbsp	*virgin olive oil*

First prepare the vinaigrette. Place the garlic, salt and some pepper in a large salad bowl. Using a wooden pestle, pound the ingredients until they break down into a paste. Add the vinegar and stir until the salt dissolves. Pour in the olive oil and mix thoroughly.

With your hands or the pestle, stir the onion slices into the vinaigrette to coat them well. Set them aside to marinate for 30 minutes.

Cross a pair of salad servers over the bottom of the bowl, to keep the dressing separate from the leaves that will be added before the salad is tossed. Lay a few of the largest lettuce leaves on the servers, then fill the bowl with the remaining lettuce and the rocket.

Top the leaves with the French beans, hard-boiled eggs, olives and basil. Draw out the servers from the bed of lettuce and rocket and toss the salad with the servers, or by hand, until all its ingredients are lightly coated with the dressing.

White Chocolate Coffee Rolls

Makes 16 rolls
Working time about 1 hour
Total time: about 2 hours (includes chilling)
Per roll: Calories 215, Protein 5g, Cholesterol 40mg, Total
fat 10g, Saturated fat 6g, Sodium 40mg

1 tbsp	*powdered gelatine*
15 cl/¹/₄ pint	*strong black coffee, cooled*
1 tsp	*Tia Maria*
250 g/8 oz	*fromage frais*
1	*genoese sponge 2 teaspoons of very strong black coffee added to uncooked batter*
300 g/10 oz	*white chocolate*
30 g/1 oz	*plain chocolate*

Sprinkle the gelatine over 2 tablespoons of the cold black coffee in a small bowl, leave it to soften for 2 minutes, then set the bowl over a saucepan of simmering water and stir until the gelatine has completely dissolved. Blend the remaining coffee with the Tia Maria and *fromage frais* in a food processor or blender until smooth. Add the gelatine solution and process for a further 20 seconds. Refrigerate the coffee cream filling until it has set—1 to 1¹/₂ hours

Using a long, sharp knife, cut through the genoese sponge horizontally to make two thin sheets of cake.

Trim off any dry crusts. Cut each sheet in half lengthwise, then cut each strip crosswise into four, to give a total of sixteen 10 by 7.5 cm (4 by 3 inch) rectangles. Place each rectangle between two sheets of non-stick parchment paper and roll it a little with a rolling pin; this will flatten the sponge and prevent it from cracking when it is rolled up with the filling.

Spread the cut side of each sponge rectangle with an even layer—about 5 mm (¹/₄ inch) deep—of the coffee filling, keeping it away from the edges Roll up each rectangle, starting from a short side, to make a tightly-rolled cake.

To ice the rolls, melt the white chocolate in a heatproof bowl set over a saucepan of simmering water. Place a roll on a metal spatula, seam side down. Hold it over the bowl of white chocolate, and spoon the chocolate over the roll, covering it completely. Place the iced roll on a sheet of parchment paper. Repeat until all the rolls have been coated.

Melt the plain chocolate over hot water as described for the white chocolate above, and spoon it into a greaseproof paper piping bag. Decorate the rolls with zigzags of fine chocolate piping. Allow the chocolate to set before serving.